THE GIANT THAT AWOKE

THE **GIANT** THAT AWOKE

THE JIM LEISHMAN STORY

JIM LEISHMAN with JOHN LLOYD

MAINSTREAM
PUBLISHING

First published in Great Britain 1990 by
MAINSTREAM PUBLISHING COMPANY (EDINBURGH) LTD
7 Albany Street
Edinburgh EH1 3UG

ISBN 1 85158 316 5 (cloth)

British Library Cataloguing in Publication Data

Leishman, Jim
   The Giant That Awoke: the Jim Leishman story.
   1. Scotland. Association football – Biographies
   I. Title   II. Lloyd, John
   796.334092

   ISBN 1-85158-316-5

Typeset in 11/13pt Times by Blackpool Typesetting Services Ltd
Printed in Great Britain by Billing & Sons Ltd, Worcester

ACKNOWLEDGMENTS

I would like to thank all the journalists, newspapers and photographers over the years, with a special thanks to the following for all their help in the preparation of this book: Caroline Sutherland, for all her careful typing; Inveralmond Community High School, Livingston, for the use of all their facilities; Duncan Simpson for the collation of all the statistics and help with all the pictures; Ian Malcolm and Dunfermline Athletic Football Club, for supplying the photographs; the seven delegates of the Dunfermline Football Supporters Federation; the *Daily Record, The Scotsman* and the *Sunday Mail*; Harry Goodwin, Malky McCormick, and Stuart Adamson of Big Country.

CONTENTS

Chapter 1

TAKING NEW IDEAS ON BOARD

I'm no longer manager of the best team in Fife
So it's time to get on with the rest of my life
My memories and achievements are in this book
I really appreciate you taking a look
I hope you enjoy remembering the past
Cause always in my heart these memories will last
To all the players I give a hearty vote of thanks
For putting up with me and my silly pranks
Dunfermline Athletic's a really great team
To be manager for seven years was a great esteem
And thanks to auld Sandy, Pip, Willie and Joe
You were always there to give things a go
To Sheila and Grace and all the rest
You'll always be to me the very best
Thank you the supporters, one and all
Lets hope the Pars stay on the ball

THURSDAY, 26 July 1990, was an ignominious day in the history of Dunfermline Athletic Football Club and the most wretched of my life. The two facts are not coincidental. On that day I told the press and the world that I wanted to be manager of the club, but that the position was not being offered to me by Mr Mel Rennie, the chairman. An era was at an end.

I went through the entire gamut of emotions in the week leading up to that final announcement: disappointment, disillusionment, disgust and despair. Around me my aims, dreams and ambitions lay shattered like a fallen goldfish bowl. Now I was flapping around like a fish out of water. Part of my life had been taken away from me.

This chapter provides me with the opportunity to give my personal view of those dark days and I will offer an insight into the events which every Scottish football fan was discussing that hot July. The crisis in the Gulf had begun, the Mo Johnston Italian affair and the attempted takeover of Hibs by Hearts were already well documented, but it was the real story behind the happenings at Dunfermline's East End Park which Scottish football supporters wanted explained. Big Jim, the wisecracking, larger-than-life, cigar-smoking, publicity conscious extrovert, had had the heart torn out of him by the club he loves. Why was it that the following month I would be watching the Norrie McCathie Testimonial match as an ordinary Pars supporter in the stand?

Only one week earlier I had been looking forward to the new season with keen anticipation. The wraps had come off the new Dunfermline Athletic strip, a candy stripe one which would remind fans of my generation of the wonderful times we had in the 1960s. The shorts and socks had changed little but the shirt had the latest baggy look and a flat collar in club colours. We had decided to go in for red, American-style numbers on a white square so that players could be easily identified at a distance. Norrie McCathie was telling reporters he thought it was "nice" but I know he favoured the jazzy, West German-style of shirt.

I had brought Andy Rhodes to Dunfermline from Oldham for £100,000 to provide cover for, and give competition to, goalkeeper Ian Westwater, as I'd been concerned for a while about the consequences if ever he were injured. I genuinely felt our Andy was potentially better than Andy Goram. I had signed Paul O'Brien from Queen's Park and Pat McAllister from Cliftonville. There was the exciting prospect of Dutchman Marcos Veerman coming on trial as well as the return of Istvan Kozma from Bordeaux, and we had signed George O'Boyle for £200,000. On top of all that, we had brought back for £100,000 Ian McCall, a crowd favourite and a player of awesome potential, and we had splashed out £150,000 on Yugoslav centre-back Milos Drizic. Although I had told reporters that our ambitions were modest – that we simply wanted to do better than last season and go at least one rung further up the ladder – I was excited at the prospect of Dunfermline having, arguably, the best squad in 20 years. The town was buzzing with expectation.

One telephone call would change everything!

On 19 July Mr Rennie rang me. Would I be able to come to a meeting at East End the following morning at nine-thirty? I was rather surprised and actually enquired whether there was bad news. Mel Rennie affirmed that there was "some good news". On my arrival, he was there with two other directors – Mr Blair Morgan and Mr Roy Woodrow. Both had joined the board in 1986, since when the club has been promoted twice and won two championships. Mr Morgan was best known for his involvement in the club's *EastEnders* record while Mr Woodrow was managing director of the lemonade firm. Vice-chairman Mr Braisby and directors Mr Walters and Dr Yellowley were to take no part in the events which followed. These directors present who now clearly controlled the club spoke for more than 90 minutes and the upshot was that they offered me the post of executive director in charge of specific duties such as public relations, marketing and running the commercial department. They felt that they had analysed my strengths carefully, they realised that I was popular with both the fans and the media, and they wanted me to be an ambassador for the club. They claimed it would be a great honour for me to become Dunfermline's first manager to be offered a directorship. I was also informed that this was "the unanimous view of the board" despite the absence at that meeting of half of the directors and the fact that I was speaking to those present as individuals as well.

It had been known to the board for some time that the co-manager role I shared with Iain Munro simply wasn't working. However this offer came as a complete shock – I had had no inkling of it. The directors did all they could to sell me the new post but it rapidly became apparent that they intended that I would have no further part in the footballing affairs of the team. Despite that, and maybe surprisingly, my first reaction was that this offer was indeed a supreme honour being bestowed on me.

The meeting lasted until 11 a.m. and it was as I left that I learned that my Dad had been rushed to hospital. By the time I got to my Mum's house, I learned that my father, who had been ill for some years, was okay. My mum was the first person to learn the news of the club's offer to me and her first reaction was similar to mine – what a great honour! She did not know the full story, of course.

I returned home to break the news to my wife and kids but even before I arrived my feelings were starting to change. Gradually it was dawning on me that I would no longer be handling and mixing with the players. Worst of all, I would not now ever be able to achieve my greatest ambition, namely to lead the Pars back into European competition after an absence of 20 years. I was beginning to feel let down. Why, I wondered, was I not being allowed to continue - no one had ever said I had not done well as boss of Dunfermline. Yes, I could understand the board's reasons for wanting to utilise my strengths as a PR man, but I could not see myself in that position at that time. Maybe if I had been given some warning of what was to be offered there would not have been the shock, disappointment and heartbreak I was to go through. It might have been that bit easier to take. Suddenly all the hard work I had put in from the early days when the club was firmly anchored in the Second Division, all the crusading visits to supporters clubs, boys' clubs, scouts, schools, social clubs and pubs to drum up enthusiasm and money for Dunfermline Athletic - everything seemed to have been a complete waste of time.

Yes, there was no denying that the honour and prestige would have been considerable for an ordinary man born and bred in Lochgelly but now I quietly examined all the plusses and minuses. I did not come to the same conclusion as the board which had carried out a similar exercise. I felt my best role was as manager and had enough confidence in my own abilities. I had now worked with two excellent coaches, even if I had had a much better working relationship with Gregor Abel than with Iain Munro. I desperately wanted to take Dunfermline a step further after consolidating our position in the Premier League. The club had changed dramatically since I had taken over in 1983, we were much more professional and better geared for attaining my great dream. The return to Europe was only what our magnificent fans deserved. I confided all of this to Mary, my wife, and she and the family and close friends like Ian Campbell backed me to the hilt.

At nine o'clock on the morning of Saturday, 21 July, Mel Rennie telephoned me at home and I told him of my decision to turn the offer of a directorship down. We met that same day and he tried to persuade me to take it. He had been a director of the club since 1971 and chairman since 1986 and he felt sure that I should grab this chance. He was disappointed that he had to leave for a wedding in Stornoway with the issue still unresolved.

On Monday, 23 July, directors Morgan and Woodrow turned up at training at Eagle Glen and did all they could in their power to persuade me to take up the directorship but I told them I was unwilling to give up my footballing duties. I felt – and still feel – that I have far too much to offer the footballing side of a club. However, it was only in that discussion with them that I realised there were no options being put to me! I maintained my stance on the matter but I left that meeting wondering if I had done the right thing! It became clear to me that I was no longer to be associated with a club I had supported, played for, coached and managed for all of 22 years. I drove around for an hour wondering if I should telephone and ask the directors if I could reconsider and accept the new position. It was proving to be the hardest decision I had to make in my career.

By this time there was press speculation that all was not well at the club. The Scottish *Daily Express* had hinted that the co-manager situation was not working out as far back as Easter, yet that season we had finished eighth in the Premier League and had reached the Skol Cup semi-final and the Scottish Cup quarter-final, only going out in the replay. The news was out by Tuesday, 24 July. "Leishman may resign" screamed the *Evening News* in large print. Yet again Mr Morgan and Mr Woodrow reiterated the situation and asked me to reconsider.

I had now made up my mind. I too had had time to analyse my own strengths and felt they were man-management, motivation and working with people.

Mr Rennie and I discussed things on the telephone again. In fact the phone kept ringing – my number has never been ex-directory – and the strain on my family became immense. It would have been tempting to put the phone off the hook but it would have been wrong to do that, wrong to hide. I had nothing to be ashamed of. Mr Rennie, who later conceded the matter had been handled badly, said he would "sort things out" on his return. But it became more and more clear to me that my decision was irrevocable.

I will never forget Thursday, 26 July. I made my farewells to the players. I removed my picture of my hero, Jock Stein, from the Athletic's training headquarters at Eagle Glen.

On meeting the press I did not want to go into all the speculation about boardroom reshuffles and power struggles. Happy memories began to flood through my mind and I'm going to relate these in the book, but the championship night when Ian McCall and Norrie McCathie ended up in the rafters and John Watson bought everyone a drink and left me to foot the bill were two that come instantly to mind. People like Norrie McCathie, John Watson, Bobby Robertson, Jimmy Bowie and Ian Westwater had meant a hell of a lot to me. My greatest regret was in not being able to say goodbye to every fan individually. We had become a big club again and they had been tremendous to me. They only gave me stick when I deserved it! I felt I still had my pride. I'm used to working seven days a week and even if that means sweeping the streets the good thing about Jim Leishman is that I never forget where I come from.

I had tried to crack a joke with each player but now I had the hardest task of all. There were a few fans outside East End and now I had to face them. A banner saying "Leishman must stay" had appeared. (Harry Melrose was later to remove it!) The bemused fans sang a few songs, I was patted on the back and in tears tried to make the two metres to my car. In those final moments my last thoughts were that now I knew how a prisoner must feel when he is going to be hanged but is not guilty!

That evening some close friends came round and we had a few drinks. I was trying to put on a brave face and told my friends I had made the best decision for Jim Leishman. Deep down in my heart, though, there were abject feelings of sorrow and hurt. I kept wondering where my future lay and whether this really was the end of my footballing career. I felt a lump in my throat.

Phone calls began to come in from the likes of Alex Smith, John Lambie, Billy McNeill, Gregor Abel, Craig Brown, Jim White and Bobby Robertson and they were all very sympathetic. Some felt it was unbelievable. Some had survived similar experiences. I was stunned and sickened by a comment attributed to Blair Morgan that I had not actually been doing the manager's job anyway for the last two years, but he claimed he had been misquoted, thereby learning a lesson in dealing with the press! What businessmen after all would keep anyone in employment who was not doing their job for that length of time?

Meanwhile the directors' statement read as follows:

Firstly, the chairman sends his most sincere apologies that he cannot attend this afternoon but as many of you know he is in Stornoway and he is attending a family wedding. The chairman has asked me to be the spokesman on his behalf and asked me to explain the present situation at East End Park.

14

For some time the board have been aware that the joint managers' position at our club has not been working. We have had many discussions during the close season and as a result of these discussions were determined to do everything within our power to keep both our managers at this club. We analysed very carefully the strengths of Jim Leishman and you will know, of course, what a charismatic figure he is with both the fans and also the media. He has also always been a tremendous ambassador for the club and for all of these reasons the board decided that Jim Leishman should be appointed as a director of the club, with specific duties dealing with PR, marketing and overall commercial activities. This decision was unique in two ways, in that Jim was to be the first manager in the 105-year history of this club to be offered such an honour and he would also have been the first executive director ever employed by this club, showing the advance of the club during the last five or six years. The decision to offer Jim this position was a unanimous one and it was also the unanimous feeling of the board that this was a tremendous achievement, recognising Jim's service to the club and also a wonderful opportunity for him in the future.

I regret to say that Jim has refused to accept the appointment and he has chosen to further his career elsewhere. It is quite clear that we do not agree with his decision but we do respect it. The board have spent the last four or five days attempting to persuade Jim to join us on the board and take Dunfermline Football Club forward in the next stages of its development. As you are obviously aware, we have been unsuccessful and it is with considerable sadness that the board accept that Jim is now to leave and follow a career elsewhere.

We salute his many achievements and recognise the wonderful effort he has given this club. He played a very signficant part in turning the club's fortunes around and leading the club from the Second Division to the Premier Division. He will always have many happy memories of Dunfermline and he will always be a welcome visitor. As a measure of the man I know that Jim Leishman will give 100 per cent support to Dunfermline Athletic next season and I hope that the fans will also get behind the team in what will be a difficult season for them.

Although the statement was a tribute to me and what I had done for the club, I was disappointed that it made no mention whatsoever of achieving the two championships, winning the Reserve League East, capturing the B.P. Youth Cup and gaining promotion to the Premier League for the first time in the club's history. I had been damned by faint praise – I was made to feel almost as if I had had no part in these achievements.

I have always been aware, naturally, of the intense loyalty and passion of Dunfermline fans, but even my breath was taken away by what happened next. "NO JIM – NO FANS" said the banner and "JIM FIXED IT FOR US – LET'S FIX IT FOR HIM" as 3,000 fans from the Federation of Dunfermline Supporters' Clubs marched from the Glen gates to East End car park. In such a short space of time and with precious little publicity, Federation secretary Phil McFadden and chairman Ken Cowan, both ably supported by Pars fanatic Stuart Adamson of Big Country, had organised one of the biggest demonstrations the town has ever witnessed.

Those events, the demonstrations and rallies, made me feel a very proud man. The march down the High Street was one of the most emotional occasions Pars fans have ever witnessed. Unfortunately they were not the emotional scenes associated with winning championships or gaining promotion to the Premier League but they were a heartfelt tribute from loyal fans to a man who had given his all for Dunfermline Athletic Football Club. My wife summed it up neatly when she turned to my daughter Kate and said, "Your Dad may have lost his job but these people are showing their gratitude and appreciation for what he achieved as manager of the club."

I felt it would be inappropriate for me to attend but I sent a letter thanking everyone involved and especially the Federation's delegates – Phil McFadden, John Fleming, Kenny Cowan, Marvyn Stewart, Joan Malcolm, Dave McGregor and Gerry Duffy – for all the hard work they had put in trying to get Jim Leishman his job back. I just wish I could have thanked all the fans personally. Letters, cards, tapes and calls were coming in in their hundreds and I'd also like to thank all the people who took the time to do that. I felt both honoured and humbled. They made me realise that all the work I had done for charity, old people, youngsters, schools, social clubs and the like had been worthwhile. They had not forgotten after all!

My friends and family did attend and the demonstration was given coverage by Radio Forth, while the *Sunday Post* devoted its entire front page to the occasion. Stuart Adamson, after a crack

Ross Bradley (club mascot) with Jim
Courtesy of Dunfermline Athletic Football Club

about "Is there anyone here from the Stornoway branch of the supporters club?" went on to criticise the "behind the doors" decision and stated that Jim Leishman had not just brought Dunfermline Athletic back to life, he had done the same for the whole town. He was glad, apparently, that he had not accepted a place on the board when it was offered to him in 1983. The fans later decided to boycott three games – the friendly against Moscow Torpedo, the Skol Cup-tie against Albion Rovers and the Premier League game with Hearts. All this public pressure, though, including demands for refunds of season tickets and resignations from the Centenary Club, still did not bring a change of heart from the board.

Then, on Wednesday, 1 August, I was invited to a three-hour meeting with the board. Morgan and Woodrow again implored me to change my mind and accept the directorship. I must admit that even then I was torturing myself with the thought, burning deep in my mind, "Should I or shouldn't I?". At the end of the meeting, though, the *status quo* remained unchanged.

By now there was intense media interest and two newspapers offered considerable sums for "exclusive" stories, but I felt that would only lead to distortion of the facts and unfairness to both myself and the club. At the press conference after that three-hour meeting I again felt quite emotional. It seemed as big a press conference as the club had ever had! To cover my feelings I turned to a local reporter and quipped: "Does this mean I will not get my blazer and flannels tomorrow?" That relieved some of the tension and I felt that both the directors and myself handled the situation well as we sat in Harry Melrose's office.

The fans were at fever pitch and again there was a painful exit out to the car. The board had made another statement saying the door would always remain open for me and the chairman urged the tremendous fans to get behind the team. An exciting season lay ahead, they said, with three internationalists, namely Kozma, Drizic and Nicholl, an under-21 cap in Sharp, the striking duo of Jack and O'Boyle, new signing Ian McCall and Mr Consistency Norrie McCathie. The statement went on to say that they had received hundreds of letters but they felt that the offer of a directorship fully recognised the contribution I had made to the club. That was to be the final statement. Significantly and conveniently Mr Braisby was on holiday, Mr Watters away on family business and

Courtesy of Dunfermline Athletic Football Club

The cake presented by Pars' disabled fans, March 1990

Dr Yellowley was unavailable for comment.

A few days later, I was out having some fun helping to train Ballingry Rovers with a friend. Then Dick Campbell had me along to Inverclyde doing a question-answer session with the kids. "How did you feel when you luckily beat Rangers in the Cup?" one youngster asked. The perisher turned out to be Wattie Smith's son! "How does it feel to be paid off?" another enquired! Offers of jobs began to pour in but all I had ever wanted to be was manager of the club with whom I'd had a lifelong affair. That had been taken from me. One day I might be proud to be a Dunfermline director, but not at present!

On 9 August media speculation intensified on the lines that I was to return as Dunfermline's manager with Iain Munro as my assistant. God knows where the leak came from but it was convincing enough to make an STV news report that morning. I was astounded by the news anyway, especially when I also found it in a national newspaper written by one of the most respected journalists in Scottish sport. He was held in such high esteem that I began to think there must be a chance. But because of the events which preceded this disclosure I was still not so sure. I was not going to allow my emotions and hopes to get carried away. All would now depend on the outcome of the directors' meeting which I was invited to attend the next day, 10 August. Deep in my heart I was praying that the reports would prove correct. That was all I had wanted from day one!

Yet again it was not to be. When I attended that meeting I was gobsmacked to learn that yet again I was only being offered the post of excecutive director. With my hopes dashed once more, my despair was bottomless.

At this time I received a telephone call from Mr Watters, the ex-chairman of the club and a man with whom I had had a close working relationship in the early days. He wanted to see me before the final meeting on 11 August. He is an extremely persuasive man and he spoke with me for all of an hour and implored me to reconsider. He began to put doubts in my mind. Had I done the right thing? We chatted about the good times and our mutual happy memories. However, I stuck to my argument that being such an integral part of the club I would find it impossible to be totally isolated from the playing side of things. In my heart of hearts I knew that to be true.

On 11 August at nine o'clock in the morning it really was the end of an era. I met the directors for the final time and gave them my decision that I felt unable to take on the job of executive director at this time.

It was obviously a very sad and trying time for Jim Leishman but no matter what was said and done in those last three weeks, I retain a great affection and loyalty to Dunfermline Athletic Football Club. It had been a tortuous decision to make – I had been up to four in the morning discussing it with Mary and I just couldn't stop the tears – but now I was leaving the club with my head held high, satisfied with what I had achieved in my seven years as manager. No one could ever take those happy memories away from me – 22 years' assocation with the one club was a long, long time. There was no way I would ever want Dunfermline to fail, despite some ludicrous reporting at the time – far too much work had been put in.

Courtesy of Dunfermline Athletic Football Club

Doug Rougvie and Rangers' Mo Johnson, January 1990

What did leave a bad taste in my mouth was the statement that the players had sent a fax to the directors from their hastily arranged pre-season tour of Ireland saying that they were solidly behind Iain Munro as manager – it smacked to me of a kangaroo court. My initial reaction, when I was led to believe that the players did not want me to continue as manager but to take up the post of executive director instead, was that I should indeed resign. I had always said that if the time came when either the fans or the players no longer wanted me to be manager, then that would be the time to go. All the same I found it so hard to believe that my players would take part in such a scheme. Never in that week had the

21

players' feelings ever been mentioned, but I had guided and encouraged them for seven years, sharing their moments of elation and despair – surely I knew them well enough to know this faxed message to the directors simply could not be true? Eventually I was to meet up with some of the players and confront them about the message. I demanded to know why they did not state their opinion to my face. I then learned the reality – indeed some of the first team players had wanted nothing to do with it! That knowledge at least lifted me once more – otherwise my feeling that I had always done right by the team would have been shattered. I can't help musing, though, over exactly what effect the receipt of that mystery fax by the directors at an important stage in our negotiations would have had . . .

Now I wanted matters to settle down so that the players could keep their minds on winning. I kept the phone off the hook all day and remained unavailable to the media. It was a relief later to get a short break in the family caravan. Some of my achievements as manager are obvious to everyone. There are two flags flying proudly above the main stand at East End. We won the Second Division Championship in 1986, something we had not done since 1926 and not too many of our fans remember the last time, and we took the First Division flag in 1989, something Dunfermline had never done before. We were enormously proud of the Scottish BP Youth Cup in 1988 and were Scottish Reserve League Champions in 1987. We not only reached two quarter-finals but when we played Rangers in the Skol Cup semi-final we hadn't reached that stage since 1968!

However there were other achievements that perhaps the fans were not always aware of – sometimes, I confess, I wasn't either – and that is where any club is indebted as I am to the likes of Duncan Simpson of the Pars programme, who files away a constant supply of updated reference details on the club. We had the longest undefeated run in the history of the club from 24 August 1985 to 26 January 1986, when we went 19 games without defeat. We had the longest run in the new First Division between 22 November 1986 and 28 February 1987 when we had 11 league games without defeat. We had, and this may surprise you, the longest undefeated run in the Premier Division when we went eight games without defeat between 23 September 1989 and 18 November 1989 and, of course, that included that evening out at Motherwell, when we went top of the Premier Division for the first time in the club's history. When we did win the Second Division Championship we had the highest number of league goals of any club in Britain. When we got to the Premier Division for the first time in 1987 we were only the second club ever to go from Division Two to the Premier League in just 12 months!

Raymond Sharp was our first player since Jim Wallace to be capped at under-21 level, when he played against Norway in November 1989. Istvan Kozma became the first Pars player to be capped since the days of Geir Karlsen. Probably everyone knows that the £200,000 for Ian McCall was our biggest club transfer fee received, while the £600,000 paid to Bordeaux to get Istvan Kozma was obviously a club record.

In 1987 we went full-time for the first time since 1976 and that was to prove a crucial factor in our subsequent success. We defeated Celtic at Parkhead for only the second time in the League and defeated Hearts twice at Tynecastle, having only won there three times before! Then there was the establishment of the greatest ever number of supporters clubs – 24 – not only all over Fife, but in Lothian, Central and Glasgow too!

I cannot adequately or objectively assess my own record of managerial success. Others must do that for me, but Duncan Simpson points out that, in strict percentage terms, I came fourth behind Willie Cunningham, Peter Wilson and Jock Stein, but as Wilson was only manager for one year he can probably be discounted. Willie Cunningham's career was highly successful but despite coming so desperately close to that Cup and League double in 1965 he left without ever having won a trophy. Many would also point out that the team he inherited from Jock Stein was vastly superior to the sides that Jock and I started out with. But Jock Stein must be Dunfermline's greatest manager. He started with a team hurtling towards the Second Division and took them on to win the Scottish Cup. I did win the two League Championships but my chance has gone to take the club back into Europe.

In terms of managerial tenure I came behind Sandy Archibald but that does not include the war period and William Knight who was manager for nine years in total. Only he surpassed my 128 wins! However I do have one record all to myself – we drew 77 games!

I am immensely proud, of course, in the revival of our attendances. When this book was first being discussed with my editor at Mainstream, he seemed to believe we were a "small club". I put him right. "We have the fifth-biggest gates in Scotland," I said. Honestly, these Killie fans! A total of 20,706 fans trickled through the turnstiles in my first season, an average of 1,090 – pathetic! In 1989-90 the league gates came to 197,804, an average of 10,989! That's an increase of 1,000 per cent in seven years. Only Aberdeen, Celtic, Hearts and Rangers could attract more than that. On 7 April 1984, just to put it in perspective, we had 358 fans for the home game with Arbroath and on 13 May 1989 we played Meadowbank, who have roughly the same drawing power, and had 12,976.

Our crowds have been consistently higher than teams in bigger centres of population and it is worth mentioning the phenomenal level of this support which clubs from larger towns and cities would love to emulate. How can one account for it? Why is it there is this fanatacism about football in the town? The easy answer, of course, would be the success. It is easy to support a club which has had two League flags in recent seasons. If you keep winning, the fans will always roll up. However, there has always been that tremendous potential and one of my aims was to tap it.

In January 1986 we were in the Second Division but Hibs expressed delight when they were drawn to meet us in the Cup because they knew what it would mean in gate receipts. Alex Ferguson surprised many by commenting on the radio that it could be the tie of the round and, in the event, 16,000 turned out with 7,000 at our end. In Division Two by 1985-86 we were playing to larger gates than most of Division One and, of course, in Division One we often had larger gates than two Premier League games.

Part of the answer lay in the fact that a generation of fans now my age or older were reared on the success of Stein, Cunningham and Farm and they were likely to return if the sleeping giant awoke. Today the Leishman barmy-army who weren't even born then have had four consecutive years of success to thrive on and if you go into any park in the district nearly all the boys and some girls will be wearing the Pars strip.

I had to gain the club publicity and by attending numerous social and charity events from the very beginning I was able to encourage or cajole people into spending their Saturday afternoons parting with their hard earned cash at our turnstiles. I had to make the people feel it was "their club". That was how the Centenary Club, which eventually not only benefited the fans but also brought £150,000 into the club, began. The facilities at East End are now excellent – the seating, the toilets, the catering, the supporters' shop, the safety measures and a convenient car park are all of a high standard. We also were one of the first clubs to have female mascots, ball girls and a crèche.

On the playing front I used a total of 90 players in official matches and the longest serving was Norrie McCathie. Duncan Simpson tells me that Trevor Smith was the most used substitute. I feel that I unearthed some exciting goal scorers and in football terms they were bought for peanuts! There was John Watson whose 85 goals cost us £300, a pint of Guinness and a pint of lager! Ross Jack cost £15,000 from Dundee and he scored 45. He had a slightly higher strike rate than John and that is quite an achievement as he generally faced a higher standard of opposition. He won the SPFA First Division Player of the Year award and ended up the second highest Premier goal scorer in 1990. Look at Craig Robertson. He came from Raith Rovers for £25,000 and was a prolific scorer for a midfielder. He was our highest goal scorer in 1987-88 and finished the highest scoring midfielder in the Premier Division.

Of my 82 outfield players only 37 did not score. We scored more goals against Raith than any other team (apologies to my friends in Kirkcaldy) while George O'Boyle's strike against Hamilton in the Cup was the only one we had against them. Rangers topped the goals against column but Raith top the non-Premier list, so that says a lot for the entertainment value of our derbies. In total 432 goals were scored, we lost 374. We never did play Hamilton in a League game while we played Queen of the South more than any other club. We also beat the Dumfries side more than any other team and suffered most defeats from Rangers. Most draws were also against Queen of the South but Hibs ran them close. St Johnstone failed to take even one point against us while the record against so-called bogey teams like Ayr and Cowdenbeath improved. We did not get one solitary win against Aberdeen unless you include the Centenary Cup match. I think my most dreaded opponents were Falkirk and East Fife who, at least statistically, gave more bother than some Premier teams.

My first statement as manager was: "I see it as my job for the moment to get the players going again and get the team back in the running – for a new manager taking over! I've decided I'm going to enjoy myself and take it from there. I hope I can get some of my enthusiasm for this club over to the players.''

I became manager on 31 October 1983, and enjoy myself I did!

Chapter 2

THE FAMILY BACKGROUND

Your family is a major part of your life
Especially if, like me, you have a rare wife
Who looks after my bairns, Jamie and Kate
Who never see me, often till late

Through times of frustration and often despair
It was always consoling to know they were there
Always cheering me up when my feelings were down
Raising a smile where there had been a frown

Friends you can pick, relations you cannot
From my heart, you're the best I could ever have got
The rest of my family, what a great bunch
Stayed by me totally when it came to the crunch

Mary and the bairns and, of course, me too
Will always remain Pars fans through and through

EVERY Dunfermline manager since the halcyon days of the 1960s when the club won the Scottish Cup twice, were Cup runners-up, reached the European Cup Winners' Cup semi-finals and quarter-finals, played frequently in the Fairs Cup and made a serious challenge for the League flag, has announced solemnly that his aim is to "awaken the sleeping giant". Sometimes the giant was briefly roused but usually it promptly dozed off again! Now the giant is wide awake and the happy days are back at East End. Since 1983 Dunfermline have become only the second club to go from Division Two to the Premier League in 12 months; two Championship flags have been unfurled; the BP Youth Cup has been gained and a return to Europe is a distinct possibility without having to go to war to achieve it!

Of course I am talking about what has become known as the "Leishman era" and it is already well documented in a plethora of excellent books. In 1985, the club's centenary year, historian and teacher John Hunter published *Dunfermline Athletic 1885-1985* in which he wrote the definitive piece of research into the club's history. Disappointed that the final chapter did not conclude with promotion, he followed that up with *Premier Bound* covering the successful period 1985-87. The same period was featured in *Leishman's Lions* by Robert Fraser and Douglas Scott's *Black and White Magic*. John Lloyd in the *Scottish Football Today* book focused on 1987-88 while many other newspapers and magazines have also tried to analyse the Leishman era.

However, I feel there has always been something missing. Only one person could give a real insight into the behind-the-scenes story. What were the experiences that shaped the character of Jim Leishman as player and manager? How was the extrovert personality developed? What were the major influences on his life? Who were the great characters? And what were the most memorable incidents during this period? Indeed how did the love affair with this provincial football team in a soccer-mad town begin! Only Jim Leishman can tell these stories, many of them unknown to the club's loyal followers and I think they add some colour to the books I have mentioned.

The certificate states that I was born to Mary on 15 November 1953, the year Everest was climbed, at 15 Gardener Street, Lochgelly, and, although some fans have called me the Dunfermline Messiah, there was no stable or three wise men! I was the youngest of four children born to my parents, Mitchell, a miner, and Mary. From the start I think football was in my blood but the family were not Pars fans. My grandparents, uncles, Mum and brother George supported Hibs. The family came from Chirnside in the Borders so that was the connection. In fact some of the first games I was taken to were at Easter Road, though at that time I was more interested in the crowd and the atmosphere than what was happening on the pitch! Maybe their attempts to get me to support the team explains my pleasure in Dunfermline attaining larger gates than Hibs in 1989-90 for the first time. My Dad was a Gers fan, and his father

Happy families

had even been a First Division referee in the 1940s. My brother Mitchell is a Celtic fan and I will never forget the day he asked me for tickets for the Dunfermline–Celtic game.

The game was actually Dunfermline's first meeting when I was in charge of the Premier League team, though it was in the Skol Cup third round. Mitchell phoned me on several occasions to obtain two tickets for the Celtic end. I refused and after two or three horrendous arguments and my trying to explain the reasons why I couldn't give him the tickets, he didn't speak to me for three or four days before the game. On the day of the match, after organising the team and making sure everything was okay for putting them on the park to play, I went out the dressing-room door and down the steps to the dugout where we always sat. At the side of the dugout was a banner reading "Leishman must go" and holding the banner, to my astonishment, was my older brother Mitchell. He and his friends had paid to get in and were waving this banner so that everyone, including the directors, could see it. We have had many laughs about it since then but on the night I think – I'm sure – that my brother was serious about the remarks he had on his placard.

My sister Elizabeth was the exception in the family as she had no great interest in the game until she came to East End when I was the Manager – then she was hooked!

The family is and always has been close-knit and although as kids we had all the usual scraps that children do, I have lots of happy memories. One of my favourites concerns my sister. She may not have shared my interest in football but like me she enjoyed a Saturday afternoon at the local flea pit. My favourite films were the *Zorro* ones. However, on this occasion she came with me to see *The Hunchback of Notre Dame*, a film she had looked forward to for ages. I went as usual with my two shillings, 1/9d for the seat and 3d for Reid's fruit. Every time Quasimodo appeared I howled until my sister had to take me out and she didn't forgive me for a very long time!

Lochgelly is a close-knit community which in the 1950s depended almost totally on the coal industry for survival. A family of four children stretched my parents' budget but my childhood was a happy one. Football was a cheap hobby and I enjoyed both that and my time at Lochgelly South and West Primary Schools. It was at the infant and then the primary school that my interest in Dunfermline Athletic began. Just as my family supported Hibs, Celtic and Rangers because of their illustrious past, so Dunfermline were beginning to make a name for themselves. In 1961 when I was just eight, a Mr Stein took them to a memorable Cup final win against all the odds, 2-0 against Celtic. I had a hero for life.

However there was no time or money to go along and watch the team all my pals were talking about. I was good at football and by the age of ten I was playing half-back in the first-year Lochgelly East.

Most Saturdays I would go along to the local park in Lochgelly to see my brother George playing for the first year Lochgelly East team. On one occasion two of the players hadn't turned up and although I was still at the primary school, Lochgelly West, my brother and some of the players asked me to play. I was very

Brothers George, Mitchell, mother Mary, sister Betty and me, presenting Raymond Sharp with the Jay Tees Supporters Young Player of the Year Trophy

nervous at the fact that it was the first time that I had probably played against lads who were bigger and stronger than myself but I donned the strip, played right-back for the team and I was so proud afterwards at having been in the Lochgelly East winning team against Kelty Public School that I couldn't wait to go home and tell my mother and father that I had played for the "big boys", as we called them then. It was a great achievement and on several occasions afterwards the lads from Lochgelly East first year were quite glad to have me in their team although I was two or three years younger.

My first manager was a tremendous character at the primary school called Mrs Reid. She was a tall woman who organised my first ever competitive game at Hill of Beath Primary School. She was so keen that she would organise the training, usually on the Wednesday afternoon. She had no clue of how to train or coach players but the enthusiasm she showed rubbed off on all the lads, I'm sure, throughout their careers. There were many happy times playing at the primary school, and even though we only played four or five games throughout the year before leaving to go to the high school and never won at all, the lads who played in that team have remained great friends throughout their lives. I'm sure Mrs Reid will be pleased to know that she guided us all and gave us a pride in playing for the team and going out and giving 105 per cent.

Many will be surprised to learn that I was playing as often in goal as in the outfield and I've never forgotten the day I let in five goals against Hill of Beath. The player who scored all five, and who has never let me forget it, was Ian Campbell whose career has frequently crossed with mine. We went on to play at under-14, under-16 and under-18 levels, and in the same Dunfermline team from 1973 to 1975 (as did his brother Dick). He returned as a player and then coach in the final push for promotion in 1986 and 1987. He says I gave up playing in goals after that 5-0 thrashing – not true! At 11 I passed the famous 11-plus and my pals were beginning to use the name by which I am best known today, "Big Leish".

However, my brains were not all in my feet. I now transferred to Beath High School where I was to gain six "O" Grades and two Higher Grades which later set me up for my job working for the Civil Service. I enjoyed school but naturally my happiest memories were of football and other sports. I became involved in scouting and ended up as assistant leader with the 33rd Fife Macainsh Church Scout Troop, where I had a great time on camping trips and rambles. I began to run the under-14 Woodmill Boys' Club and was gaining an insight into leadership which was perhaps a factor in my eventually becoming a school prefect.

I was already physically big, good at any sport I turned my hand to. I won numerous races on Sports Day. However, I was never one to crow about my achievements and this attitude, which has stuck with me all my life, was reinforced by an incident one day at high school. There was a boy in the school who was one year older, an international schools footballer. Although he was outstanding he was given a real rollicking one day by a teacher I respected, a Mr Hutchinson. "You'll never be half the man Jim Leishman is," he roared. "You don't have the right attitude or commitment!" I learned a lesson myself that day. Don't shout about your achievements, let people notice and they'll give you the credit. Always remember too that other people matter. I have never forgotten that.

I was always organising football matches, usually eight-a-side against teams like St Pat's in Lochgelly. However, the craziest of all were Brucefield Celtic and Brucefield Rangers on a Sunday. The teams hardly ever changed because they were based naturally on which half of the Old Firm you supported. There were any number of players and the game was played for a silver paper cup made out of silver paper taken out of a cigarette packet. It was a cardboard cup with all the silver paper squashed together and made to look like the Scottish Cup.

Probably some of the best times I ever had as a youngster were experienced while playing for Brucefield Rangers. Ally Bird and George Bird, two brothers who organised the games, were fanatical Old Firm supporters, except that Ally supported Celtic and George supported Rangers. On Sunday mornings everyone went down to the Brucefield Park for ten o'clock when the team selections were made. Luckily, I was good enough to get a game every week and started playing for Brucefield Rangers. The seriousness and dedication that was put in by both teams I'm sure was often greater than the real thing of the Old Firm games! Everyone had to sign papers to say they were officially a Brucefield Rangers or a Brucefield Celtic player; there was no tapping and transfers had to be approached through the managers. For example, if Ally wanted to buy or transfer one of his players to or from his brother George they had to apply in writing and have meetings. It was so serious that even before some games they argued which way they were kicking because of the Brucefield slope! Each half lasted an hour and at half time you dashed home for stew and tatties!

All the time I had the backing, support and encouragement of my Dad, Mitchell. I'm sure that I inherited my extrovert nature from him. He was always cheery and outgoing, he loved a party and was always the first to stand up and sing, usually *Stornoway*. When I began to play for Townhill Boys' Club, a really successful team which won the West Fife Cup and League and every trophy at under-16 level, he was always there to support me and give advice. When we won the under-16 Scottish Juvenile Cup the *Sports Pink* had the headline, "Leishman was a tower of strength", and he was as proud as me. It was a great day in his life when Dunfermline chief scout Andy Young knocked at my door. Though my Dad watched me as a Dunfermline player, it is my greatest regret that he had a heart attack shortly after I became Dunfermline manager which prevented him from moving too far from the house and meant he could not witness at first hand my subsequent achievements.

33

Although my first, albeit vague, recollection of a match at East End was the thrilling 6-2 defeat of Valencia in 1962, by 1966 and 1967 I was a fanatical Dunfermline supporter in the period which was to culminate in Dunfermline winning the Scottish Cup for the second time, under George Farm. Players like Roy Barry, Willie Callaghan, John Lunn and Jim Fraser were now my heroes and, not surprisingly, this posed a real problem. Dunfermline frequently played major European games in midweek and that meant a long walk or sometimes a lift to a match from Lochgelly. I liked History but found the Higher Grade hard going – and what should be on each Wednesday in the afternoon's last two periods but that subject! The Janitor used to always be looking for volunteers to help him tidy the school playgrounds, and every time Dunfermline had a midweek game I used to volunteer as I knew I only had to go round to where the lessons were, look busy for five or ten minutes, and catch assistant rector Harry McNaughton's attention. As soon as he noticed that I was doing this type of job I would disappear quietly from the school by jumping over the fence, heading up the cuddy road from Cowdenbeath to East End Park, hoping to catch a lift before the teachers eventually finished at school and saw me walking to East End Park. Four or five times I did this and I'm sure to this day Harry McNaughton has never found out.

I had been called "Puskas" by my family and friends when I played football on family holidays in Chirnside and was now winning Scottish Amateur Caps when Peter Rice was in charge. I gained two Scottish Schoolboy caps and also three caps for the Scottish Youth team. Amongst my contemporaries were such names as Pettigrew, McNaughton, Filippi, Burns, Stewart, Scott, Mackie, Johnstone, the two Grays and Anderson. I signed professionally for Dunfermline Athletic on 3 June 1971.

This was one of the most exciting events of my life and I can remember vividly not being able to sleep the previous night, as I lay in my bed wondering how I would face up to meeting some of my all time great heroes such as Roy Barry, John Lunne, Willie Callaghan, people who had played in the semi-final of the European Cup Winners' Cup only two years previously. I remember getting up at six a.m. and having a shave, wash, the normal things that one does. I remember sitting from seven a.m. to nine a.m. waiting for the bus to arrive, probably the two longest hours ever! It seemed an eternity before I would be gracing the hallowed turf

Eat your heart out, George Best: Jim and Mary in 1978

at East End Park. I waited and waited and then just before the bus was to arrive I realised I had left a pair of boots in the house. I thought I had enough time to rush back, get the new boots, and return in time to catch the bus. Unfortunately when I came back I saw it leaving and instead of being early for training I knew that I was going to be at least an hour late on my first day. What would Alec Wright think! Luckily Andy Young, who had seen me as a school boy, was passing in his car. He stopped and after ten minutes of shouting and bawling at me about being late on my first day as a professional football player we arrived at East End Park.

When I entered the Stadium feeling so proud, my second mistake was walking into the first-team dressing-room where I met with five-foot-six Andy Stevenson, who also shouted and bawled and told me that when I was good enough to get into the dressing-room on merit that is when I should come in. I felt embarrassed but it made me more determined to get into the first team as quickly as possible. Obviously, that was where the action was to be.

But by now a new influence was entering my life. I first met my wife Mary in the Kinema Ballroom at the age of 17, when I took her home but apparently didn't impress her. I thought I was the "bee's knees", the best player in the world. She probably considered me a pain in the bum! We didn't meet again until I was 22, at a function at the Glen Pavilion run by Philips where I was guest of honour presenting awards. We were reintroduced through a mutual friend and although she had no great interest in football she persuaded me to marry her! If she contests this she can write her own book one day!

Strangely, it was to be me that got really hooked on her hobby – musicals. Mary, you see, is the star of the musicals performed by Kelty Amateur Operatic in Dunfermline's Carnegie Hall. At the time Mary and I were going out, the president of the musical society was her father Jock. The musical director was after someone to play Big Jule in *Guys and Dolls*. The person he was looking for had to be big, tough and ugly and appear stupid – guess who got the part? I was more nervous on the first night in front of 600 souls than I had ever been facing 47,000 at Parkhead. I remember being sick three times. But I loved it and went on to play Stewpot in *South Pacific*, Sitting Bull in *Annie Get Your Gun*, Black Eagle in *Rose Marie* and a variety of small parts. However I was always acting rather than singing and when I tried to play Ali Hakham in *Oklahoma*, I ended up speaking songs long before Telly Savalas ever did.

Mary and I were married in Kelty Church in 1979 and football friends like Alan Evans and Graham Shaw attended. My best man was Jock Petrie, a school chum. We were too early in arriving at the church and ended up, rather conspicuously in top hat and tails, drinking a beer in the Oakfield Bar. We were so nervous going to the church we each had miniatures of whisky in our top hats hidden by the gloves! As we walked up to the church I tripped just as I was being cine-filmed for posterity. How will I ever forget it?

It was a great day, though, and we have been blessed with Kate, born in May 1981, and Jamie, in September 1987. I'll never forget Kate's birth. I was playing Stewpot in the musical and, as the baby was due on the last day of the week-long run, Mary was not taking part. However Mary was a week overdue. With nothing happening, we attended the usual wild last night party and got to bed at three in the morning. At six she gave me a nudge. Her labour had started. The drive to the maternity home with the adrenalin flowing was one I'll never forget. Jamie could have been born on a match day and I had already made the decision to put family before football but,

Rogues gallery corner

in the event, he was born midweek and there wasn't a game on. Once the kids came on the scene we became a two-car family. I couldn't get a pregnant Mary into the Fiat 126!

Both our children have extrovert natures. Jamie is hyperactive but I want him to develop his own personality. There is no question whatever of steering him towards a career in football. Kate is into

37

singing, dance (her Gran is a dancing teacher for the musicals) and karate and she is a real poser. She howled when there was all the media coverage when I became DAFC Manager because the cameraman hadn't photographed her. Since those days she has revelled in being the child of someone in the public's eye.

A family is so important, especially when you are under the type of pressure I was in in the last week of July 1990. On the evening before I finally resigned as Dunfermline's manager, I went home after my meeting with the directors. As on previous nights my house was full of family and close friends – some ten or 15 people all sitting waiting for me to tell them the outcome of the meeting. I told everyone that I had finally decided not to take the vacancy on offer as executive director and that on the next day I would be making a statement to the Press to that effect.

They all consoled me and we decided to have a few drinks. Out came the brandy, whisky and vodka and by the time the drink had been flowing for a few hours and something like normal service was being resumed my friend Brian Marr called for order and announced, "Okay, let's have a sing-song but the rules are that you must relate the song that you sing to Big Jim." He kicked off by giving us an emotional rendition of *You'll Never Walk Alone*, I stood up and sang *Please Release Me, Let Me Go* and Mary replied with *You're Free To Go, Darling*! We all had a good laugh but after another few songs my daughter Kate whispered to me, "Dad, can I sing a song? I've got a song I'd like to sing."

So, I asked everyone to be quiet and give the best of order for my nine-year-old girl Kate who would like to sing a song to her Dad. I must admit I felt so proud at just that moment. I even had a glint of a tear in my eye. Kate stood up and the room fell silent in anticipation. She then raised her hand and started waving, singing *Cheerio, Cheerio, Cheerio*!

The room collapsed with laughter. We were literally rolling about the house and I'm sure the noise could be heard all the way to Dunfermline. I immediately chased Kate round the house and stopped her pocket money for three weeks. Only joking!

But I must also state here that at this particular time in the resignation saga both my in-laws, John and Lena, were of great support. No matter what was going to happen they would stick by us through thick and thin, as they always had done, giving us hope, advice and encouragement.

*John, Lena and Mary along with Black Eagle in Kelty Musical's
production of* Rose Marie

Another memory is after the shattering 5-0 Skol Cup semi-final
defeat by Rangers, when we had all expected great things. I came
home shattered and mentally drained. The following morning
Jamie came into our bedroom and I was still wallowing in self-pity.
True to form, he spilled his juice all over the bed. A family certainly
brings you straight back to reality and that is really important. If
you are getting too big for your boots a family soon puts a stop to
it and, if they don't, Lochgelly people certainly do. I am one of their
own and they treat everyone alike. Sometimes a family helps to talk
out a problem, like was a team selection wrong? Did certain
individuals play badly? At other times they sense when to say
nothing!

I love being accessible to fans and the media. My phone number
is in the book and I will talk to anyone anywhere who is keen on
the game or the club. But it is so nice to get back to my home in
Keltybridge, to relax with friends and family, to have some peace
and then recharge the batteries. As Dunfermline Athletic manager
I lived near my employment and the kids are at an excellent local
school. Like all families we have differences of opinion and different tastes. I watch wildlife, sport and nature programmes on
television when Mary is in another room watching *Neighbours*,

39

Cheers or *The Golden Girls* and Kate is somewhere else entirely. Musically, I enjoy Nazareth, Big Country (both Dunfermline bands), Average White Band or The Doobie Brothers whereas Mary puts on an LP like *Oklahoma* while she is cooking. We like Italian or Chinese food but do not have an expensive lifestyle. Certainly we can afford to go abroad yet our idea of real fun is a break at Pettycur caravan site.

I have a strong belief in God and there have been many times when I have said a quiet prayer. Visiting Jerusalem and Bethlehem had a lasting effect on both of us. I said a few prayers, I admit, during the final crisis at East End but God had rather more important disasters to deal with. Our religious belief explains too our love of Christmas – a real family time. Like most families the annual get-together is unchanging. On Christmas Eve we take presents to my parents at Lumphinnans Road. Later my friends Brian Marr and Bill Smart come round and "prepare for Santa" by putting the milk and biscuits out for the reindeer. Once the kids are up, Christmas is in full swing. All the family comes round for the meal and we play games and sing songs. I stay up for the bells at Hogmanay with Dad and Mum but normally New Year is quiet as footballers are still working when everyone else is enjoying themselves. We could do with a two-week winter shut down!

I hope I have explained in this chapter how my character developed. I think I have disproved the saying "Give me a child for the first seven years and I'll give you the man". My nature developed then, certainly, but my love of Dunfermline Athletic Football Club came in my teens.

Then, sensibly, I did not smoke. The final piece in any jigsaw of "Mr Dunfermline" must be my large cigars. I hadn't smoked till January 1984 when we lost 2-1 in a sensational Cup-tie at Ibrox. It was the match which, in retrospect, was the turning point for Dunfermline Athletic, as any fan there that day will testify. Bill Baxter, then in charge of the reserves, gave me five King Edwards. I took one when Rab Stewart scored the opening goal for us and then I chainsmoked as Rangers, disbelievingly facing their worst defeat since Berwick, piled on the pressure. It was agonising! John Watson and Kevin Hepburn were on the bench and I sent John on. Suddenly my cigar fell somewhere on the trackside, so I sent Kevin out to warm up and told him he wasn't getting on till he found it!

Mum and Dad's Silver Wedding

Incidentally, Jock Wallace's team won 2-1 and Stephen Morrison got the Superfit award. Jock admitted afterwards he had been worried. He also told me my defensive tactics had been great. Impressed, I tried the same plan a week later in the Second Division and it was a complete disaster! But I was learning and my willingness to learn is the most important aspect of my personality.

Chapter 3

JIM, THE PLAYER

As a youngster I played with the Boys Club Townhill
Won every game including the Scottish, now that was a thrill
Signed for Dunfermline as a schoolboy, the year was '68
It was an honour to do so, I really felt great
Then signed professional, season '70/71
The hard work just starting but it was good fun
I was strong in the tackle and good in the air
Quick over the ground and played with a bit flair
Passing the ball, never knew where it would land
Often out the park, sometimes over the stand
One hundred per cent effort you always got from me
And if you're a Pars fan I'm sure you'd agree
Loyalty and commitment I gave like the rest
No other team for me, 'cause I played for the best

ONE of the proudest moments of my life was the unforgettable day when Andy Young, Dunfermline's Chief Scout (the man responsible for bringing Thomson, Wallace, Mercer, Mackie, Shaw, Robertson, Evans and Paterson to East End) knocked on my parents' door and asked if I would like to sign an "S" form for Dunfermline Athletic. I was not yet 15 and it didn't take much thinking about! I still played for Townhill Boys Club, who at under-16 level were tremendous Scottish Cup prospects, and for the Dunfermline Youth team under 18s. I had one year with Dunfermline United, the outstanding nursery team (so outstanding that the Townhill Manager, Jock Thomson, the famous sprint coach, and father of Kenny, was none to pleased about the competition!) and was called up as a player on 3 June 1971. When I left East End in July 1990 I had been there for 22 years.

In 1968 Dunfermline Athletic were at their peak. Today's youngsters can hardly imagine just how big they were in fact. Mention the participation of Scottish clubs in Europe and people tend to think of the Old Firm winning the European Cup and Cup Winners' Cup, of Aberdeen's famous victory in Gothenburg or of the magnificent consistency of Dundee United, yet before many of these clubs competed on the continent Dunfermline's name was as well known across Europe as Rangers is today! It is history, of course, that my hero Jock Stein had taken the club to a sensational Cup win over Celtic in 1961 and that gained entry into Europe. The Cup final crowd was 113,228, the biggest that will ever watch the Pars. Stein had taken over a club on the verge of relegation, a yo-yo team. There were six games left in the season and the Athletic had to win them all. Jock claimed he didn't have a magic wand but with that masterful blend of tactics and psychology which would become

Slim Jim 1969/70

43

his hallmark he inspired the Pars who won the lot. Suddenly the club went from being a very ordinary Division Two club with a mediocre ground and a lack of ambition to match, to being an established First Division club challenging for League, Cup and European honours and with a stadium to match, a stadium which to this day remains a monument to his memory. In the years which followed, the Pars played twice in the European Cup Winners' Cup and five times in the Inter Cities Fairs Cup, the forerunner of today's UEFA Cup. "Who are Dunfermline?" the Everton Manager enquired in 1962 when his team came out of the hat in round one in the Fairs Cup. He soon learned! They were dismissed 2-1 and my first match as a fan was Valencia in the next round. The last Pars appearance in Europe was in 1970 against Anderlecht of Belgium, when we went out on a 3-3 scoreline, dismissed on the away goals rule. Once I was appointed Manager the wish to see the return of those days when the Saltire flew proudly over East End on a cold and frosty evening became my greatest driving force. I was brushed aside before I had the opportunity to achieve that goal.

However, as Jim Leishman, the impressionable youngster from Lochgelly, stood outside the East End on his first day as a player in 1968, gazing at the awe-inspiring stadium, the club wasn't only doing well in Europe. They had won the Scottish Cup and would do so again that year. They twice came third in the 1960s in the old Division One and in 1965 only just missed the double when they lost the Cup final 2-3 to Celtic in one of the greatest finals ever and missed out on the championship by a mere point! George Farm, the ex-Blackpool goalkeeper, was Manager, Andy Young coached the youngsters (he had been the Scottish Scout for Leeds United and turned down the Manager's seat at Cowdenbeath to become the great talent spotter I've already described) and the board had embarked on an ambitious plan to set up under-18 and under-16 teams, which in due course would feed the local talent through to the first team. Joe Nelson (who's been at East End forever – sorry, Joe!) helped behind the scenes.

The players at the club in 1968 were my heroes. The Cup final team was Martin, Callaghan, Lunn, McCarty, Barry, T. Callaghan, Lister, Paton, Gardner, Robertson and Edwards. Roy Barry, the captain and uncompromising centre-back, was the greatest of them all. It's a measure of his fame that Old Firm fans sang about him – even when the Pars weren't in opposition! By the

Spot the goalie, 1967

time I was called up in June 1971 the club was suddenly in decline. In 1969 they had finished third in the league and reached the European Cup Winners' Cup semi-final but by 1970 they were in ninth place and in 1971 they dodged relegation by the skin of their teeth. An era was at an end. I was not fully aware of what was actually happening behind the scenes, nor was I aware how near to bankruptcy the club had come. I now know that in that successful period the club had plugged a fortune into ground improvements, had only sold a player if they were offered monopoly money, while Stein, Cunningham and Farm signed talented players at bargain prices from other league clubs or by superb scouting from local junior teams. They managed to compete with the Old Firm with huge wages and bonuses.

A myth has grown up that the Pars always played to huge gates. In reality, some European games failed to get 10,000 and some foreign trips worked at a loss. Today's average gate at East End compares favourably with that period. With consecutive poor seasons, no challenge for honours and gate receipts failing to keep

45

up with expensive transfer fees, the alarm bells began to sound. A public appeal began, to avert the fate which befell Third Lanark, and among the new directors was one Mel Rennie. I remember one crazy Edinburgh businessman, John Kidd, gaining publicity by saying he would take over the club and have the players out training mornings, afternoons and evenings! "What do these guys know about football?" the young Leishman asked!

By 1971 there were still 28 full-timers at the club but, as the financial crisis continued, there was no money any more to splash out on new players. The club had to hope and pray that the Youth policy had worked and that youngsters like me would mature quickly enough for the club to survive. This didn't seem at all optimistic to me. Along with Jim Paterson, Gordon Pate, Peter Brown, David Stobie and Robert Marshall I had been included in the Scottish under-18 Schoolboy side and I felt I was destined for stardom. The Manager now was Alex Wright, the former St Mirren Manager and Partick player. As a youngster I had not had too much contact with George Farm but I do remember that he was always very fair with me. He had persuaded my Dad that I had a great future at the club when teams like Newcastle were taking an interest. However, Farm was an awesome character. During practice sessions he would really bawl and shout at the players.

His attitudes also influenced the rest of the coaching staff. Now and again youngsters like me were allowed to train with the big name professionals. We would strip in the away dressing-room and wait for trainer Andy Stevenson to call us out at 20-minute intervals to take our turn. I used to quake, my knees knocking together waiting for the call. I had learned from the very beginning that I was not allowed in the home dressing-room. On my very first day as a full-timer I walked through the players' entrance with my polished boots under my arm. I opened the home dressing-room door and met an irate Andy Stevenson. "Get bloody out of here," he yelled. "Get to your own dressing room. You'll get back in here when you are good enough!"

Under Alex Wright, Willie Maclean was the new trainer and each day the squad was large enough to have two teams. I was put in my place from the start. The proud captain of the Scottish Schoolboys team had to act as ballboy! The club was having to cut its coat according to its cloth but players still had a three-course lunch at the Regal restaurant after a hard training session. However

Jim Leishman celebrates a Pars win over Hearts

I recall there was a lot of pressure. We were still regarded as a top European team, the local people expected good results and dodging relegation in 1971 was regarded as a blip in an otherwise successful period. This was to prove misplaced optimism. In 1971-2 we would be relegated, coming bottom of the league on 23 points and today the season is probably only remembered for Alex Wright, Jim Fraser and John Cushley winning *Quiz Ball,* the wonderful football and general knowledge quiz the BBC ran and which in my view was axed prematurely. There are many clever footballers today like Malpas, Bannon and Irons who could really display their talents.

Very few of the Cup stars were left by the time the team photo was taken in that August. The average age of the squad was only 22 and only Joe McBride was over 30. As the season went on, more experienced players left and youngsters were given their head. In the September Alex Wright had Pat Gardner, George O'Neill and Jim Brown injured. Unknown to me he had decided to gamble on bringing me into the team for the match with Ayr United at Somerset Park. I was at home shaving when my photo appeared on screen in the football preview. My parents roared at me to come into the lounge and I cut myself so badly in my excitement that I looked like a character from a Hammer horror movie as I screamed in front of the set!

I played my part in a vital 1-1 draw and was over the moon when Alex and captain John Cushley, who had talked me through the game, praised me afterwards. I was only to play seven games that season, one as a substitute, but no player forgets his first goal and, playing in midfield, I got two that season. My first came on Saturday, 22 April 1972, against Clyde at East End. Wearing the number six shirt, I went up for a corner and headed the second goal in 62 minutes. Well, I ran across to the enclosure directly opposite the stand, where the hardcore fans have traditionally congregated. All the other players fell on top of me in congratulation and we all picked ourselves up and ran to the centre spot. Then, as the loud cheering continued, I ran back again to accept the crowd's acclaim! I was just a raw, excited laddie and, in retrospect, they must have thought I was cracked. Five days later, on the 27th, at Ibrox, I scored what some regarded as the best goal a Pars player has ever scored there. With the score at 3-3 I took the ball in the inside right position and beat two defenders before crashing a left-foot shot past 'keeper Peter McCloy to give Dunfermline a mighty rare away win against Rangers.

Of course, by then, it was extremely rare for Athletic to appear in front of the cameras. Indeed until I became Manager in the 1980s about the only way you could get the Pars on your television screen was to rent out the video of the club's greatest 1960s games. Well, be sheer chance that debut match against Ayr was televised. I was out celebrating that evening, and met and brought back this attractive young lady. To show off, I propped her in front of my television at home in time for match highlights. Minutes before the game was due to broadcast, there was an announcement that, due to unforseen circumstances, the match couldn't be shown that evening! My pals never let me forget it.

I was starting to regard myself as a real star and I must have been a real poser with my long black hair and ludicrous crocodile shoes. My £80 a week pay was huge by the standards of the day. I also enjoyed being recognised in the street. My name was headline news on the back of every paper after the goal against Rangers so every Celtic fan in Lochgelly was my friend that month. But I can't write what the Gers fans shouted at me!

One person who had a great influence on me that season was Joe McBride, who had also been a star at Celtic and Hibs. Most of my games were in the reserves and latterly that was where you found these great names of the past. Once we were in the same team to play against East Fife reserves at East End and Alex Edwards was totally despondent at being named for the second team. He was still a top-class player and had played at the highest level. McBride immediately cottoned on that his attitude was not right and collared him before he left the dressing-room. "If you want a move you must snap out of this attitude," he snarled. "Stop all this huffing and puffing. Contribute to the game and get your act together!" Alex Edwards had five youth caps, an amateur international cap and under-23 caps and was one of the best Dunfermline players of all time but he was totally unsettled. He was a real steal for Hibs at £13,000!

Another memory from that period was playing left-back for the reserves at Parkhead and not immediately realising just who the "Johnstone" was that I would be marking. As the teams came out, I suddenly realised it was "Jinky" himself. It was one of my highlights to play – and win – against such a star.

My final reminiscence from that season is not one I recall with any pleasure. My goal against the Gers had given us a lifeline at the end of 1972 and only a win against a Dundee United side at East End would keep us up. We were in this mess because basically all the star names had grown old together and the club was in no position to go out and buy star replacements. It wasn't all gloom however. In late February George Miller became Manager and his influence on me was to be immense. A youngster called Ken Mackie had an incredible debut against Hibs when we defeated them 2-1 at home, then Graham Shaw played his first game at Dundee. We didn't know it then but a devastating partnership was in the making. It couldn't save us, though. We lost 0-1 to a United team with a new young manager called Jim McLean, and a crowd of 8,500 saw us relegated for the first time since 1958. No one played well that day and in the dressing-room afterwards we were all gutted, although I concede that it was the older players, who had known the good old days, who were really devastated. Barrie Mitchell, something of a hero, and top scorer with eight goals was transferred to Aberdeen for £25,000 and made an inopportune remark about how tough it was that we were being relegated. We knew he did not have any of our worries about the decline in living standards or the possibility of even a free transfer and, frankly, he was lucky to escape with his life! Being relegated is an awful feeling.

Neil Kinnock, once told a Labour Conference, "Remember how you felt after the Conservatives won the General Election?" Well we felt the same and I did not intend ever having to repeat that particular experience.

Season 1972-73 was not going to be easy. As we trooped out in the sun for the annual team photo, only Willie Callaghan, who would soon move to Harry Melrose's Berwick and John Lunn, who tragically would have to give up the game after 11 magnificent seasons, survived out of the Cup team. The full-timers were reduced to only 16. Andy Young left when the youth teams were scrapped and even Humbug Park was sold in an attempt to make economies. George Miller was truly brilliant at delving into the free transfer market and the best of these were Dundee's Alex Kinninmonth and Joe Hughes on an exchange deal from East Fife.

It was also good to get back to the real candy stripe Dunfermline strip, which I would bring back to the club as Manager after a number of variations in 1990. But we just had to get back into the First Division. Gates were at 2,000 to 5,000 and ominously the board stated that we needed 12,000 to break even. It would eventually result, just after I left, in part-time football and it would take the club years to recover from that decision.

I was to be a regular in the team that season, playing in a total of 34 games and scoring twice. The other stalwarts that year were Arrol in goal, Wallace, Thomson, whose Dad came up to help in the training, McNicholl, Kinninmonth, Nelson, Scott, Mackie and Shaw, Hughes and Gillespie. It was to be some season. We scored an astonishing 95 goals, got promoted, won 23 games and came second to Clyde on 52 points. I've therefore experienced both promotion and relegation as both player and Manager!

George Miller, a former Dunfermline star himself, of course, and a member of the 1961 Cup-winning side, was a fantastic Manager who studied the training and coaching methods of European champions Ajax, the Dutch team. Not surprisingly, he turned us into an attacking team. I do not mind admitting that I've probably subconsciously modelled myself on him. We both had a mining family background and both loved the club intensely. He was cheery and approachable and never spoke down to people and he could motivate. He also knew the psychological approach. That sounds very abstract but I'll give what I believe is an excellent example of it.

One of the most memorable games that season was a 2-0 win at a packed Ochilview. We came out on to the pitch on a bitter, frosty afternoon wearing light blue tracksuit bottoms under our shorts and stockings. In the dressing-room there had already been cracks about doing a pirouette rather than a turn! As we came out on to the pitch we were met with so much banter and took so much stick, including wolf whistles, that we got all fired up. No wonder we won so convincingly! We kept that experiment going all through that harsh winter.

George was inspired, too, in his choice of Alex Kinninmonth as captain. He had been a great player at Dundee and had looked after himself well. He was a considerable help and encouragement to young players, he knew precisely when to praise or cajole, he was an inspirational leader and he talked us to victory many times. He was also a great person in the dressing-room. As Manager at East End, I would have liked to have had him as my number two but by then he was comitted to Raith Rovers. But he helped me as a player just as much as John Cushley did in the reserves.

Most fans will think of that season as belonging to Graham Shaw and Ken Mackie and rightly so. Graham scored 27 goals to become top goalscorer and Ken accounted for another 21. They were very different players, though. Graham Shaw had in common with the great Kevin Keegan the fact that he had to work very hard at his game. If he had been two yards quicker I honestly believe he could have played for Scotland. As it was he had a great career in the game and played in a Cup final for Hearts.

I didn't know Ken's real name for the first six months I played with him. Everyone called him Jock! He was a big, raw youngster with massive potential which was to be sadly unfulfilled. A great tanner ba' player, he was a natural who played frequently for the Scotland professional team. His skill and goals caught the attention of the mighty Rangers and an offer of £20,000 plus Penman was turned down by the board, who were desperate for cash. Eventually a bid of £50,000 came in. But, like Ian McCall in a later era, he rejected it. The other players couldn't believe it. Here was an opportunity for massive wages, honours, a wonderful standard of living, media coverage, the lot. Unlike Ian, though, nothing would change his mind. He was a big fish in a small pond and wanted to gain more experience with a provincial club. Money was just not important to Ken and that was to his credit.

Who could forget winger Jim Gillespie? The fans used to say that, if they had ever opened the gates during a match, he wouldn't have stopped running till he got to Cowdenbeath! Uncompromising defenders Jim Scott and Bonar Mercer were also great friends. At the end of the season we toured Norway but after that it would be a long time till a Dunfermline team played on European soil again.

In 1973-74 I made 40 appearances for the club and again scored two goals. We all knew that it was going to be a very difficult season back in the top division and George Miller would have to draw on all his experience to keep us there. We made it in the end, surviving by the skin of our teeth on goal difference from East Fife. We had gone bottom of the division after five successive defeats but with Falkirk already doomed, East Fife, who were two points ahead, lost, and a Graham Shaw goal gave us the miracle. We knew a Premier League was coming and we were desperate to be part of it. Hence the relief!

The season provided some truly memorable moments. The team needed experience and Jackie Sinclair returned after a magnificent

Willie Ormond, presenting team captain, Jim Leishman, with Musselburgh Five's Trophy. DFC won three years in a row

Pre-season training, 1973

career at Leicester and Newcastle. His splendid goal in the opening minutes against St Mirren beat Jim Heriot and was one of the greatest ever seen at East End. I gave him the pass on the halfway line, he took a couple of strides and unleased an unforgettable rocket. We lost 2-3 in a great game at home to Celtic and the atmosphere and media coverage strengthened my resolve that one day the halcyon days must return.

I will never forget the 2-2 draw with Rangers either. I won the Player of the Match award but the older fans will probably better recall Ian Campbell's corner volleyed home by Alex Kinninmonth. Derek Parlane was the big star in those days and my Dad told me the morning of the game, "He's not a better man than you." It's something I've said to my players on occasion since. The result made up in some way for an awful 1-6 thrashing we endured later at the hands of the same Rangers. Mind you, every cloud has a silver lining. I ended up on holiday in Tunisia as a result of it, because

George Miller won a competition to guess the three highest goalscoring teams in Great Britain that day. By sheer chance he won the prize. He couldn't go and, as I was injured, I had a lovely holiday!

Our pleasure at an amazing 5-1 victory at Dundee was extinguished by the death of John Lunn. He was one of the bravest players I have ever met. Yes, Roy Barry was my hero, I respected Jim Fraser, whose attitude at not getting a Cup final place was an example to all, and I admired the likes of the Callaghans, but John's courage singled him out. Desperately ill, he had been forced to give up the game, only to return and fight his way back into the first team. He was an easy player to get on with and a great joker yet, on a Saturday, he took his game seriously and did not suffer fools gladly. On one occasion Roy Barry was sent off – after he and John fell out during a home game! But John was modest, unassuming and liked by all. He was a great tackler and known for his goal line clearances. The following November a huge crowd paid homage to him when a Dunfermline side drew 3-3 with an Old Firm combination which included Denis Law.

This was the period of the power cuts, hence the reason we met Falkirk in the Cup on a Sunday with a few folk outside threatening us with God's wrath! We drew 2-2 and my pal Ian Campbell notched the winner in the replay. I remember it because one of our opponents was one Gregor Abel. Our paths were to cross again!

One or two of my opponents then also come to mind. One day we were to play Hearts and that meant marking World Cup star Donald Ford – not the easiest task. He was playing really well. On the day of the game, George Miller took me to one side and explained, "You are going to have to mark him tight." "How do you mean exactly?" I asked. "Put it this way," came the reply, "if Donald goes for a crap, hold the toilet paper!" During the game I tackled Donald so hard he landed on his backside. Ford was so quick and sharp that I wanted him to know I was there. Minutes later there was a thud. I had been hit on the side of my face. "That's from Donald," Drew Busby grinned!

The hardest player to stop in those days was Dixie Deans of Celtic. He twisted and turned, was brilliant in the air and was perhaps the highest scorer in the weeks prior to the game with us. George Miller called me into his office on the Friday. "Mark him tight," he demanded again. "Push, shove, do anything!" In the

What a body?

event he scored three in the first 13 minutes, one of which was a flick, turn and volley that I still don't believe. I never dared look at the dugout for the remainder of the half. I knew I was in for it.

John Greig was another tough opponent. The first time I played against him I dared to up-end him. It's not something you do twice. Shortly afterwards I was pushed into the red blaze track with the grit cutting into my hands. "Well, you started it," John smiled!

The Chairman told us 1974-75 would be a vital season because we had to gain a place in the new Premier League, a feat which a Pars team in their heyday would have found a complete formality. Ralph Brand came as coach. I would soon be indebted to him. I only made three appearances, all in the League Cup. In a midweek match, 21 August 1974, we were playing Hearts at East End. After about 20 minutes I was in a terrible collision with Jim Jeffries. I lay in agony with the referee shouting at me to get up! I called Dick Campbell, who saw I was in distress. Immediately he put this stinking, sweaty shinguard between my teeth! I forgot my leg that instant! To be serious, though, my leg was broken in three places. I was only 20.

I had lots of cards and well-wishers and I could not have been looked after better anywhere than West Fife Hospital. I had operations and the horror of pins put in to straighten my leg, but Ralph Brand worked on me and gave me every encouragement.

I can remember at the time when I broke my leg my weight was eleven stone six pounds and after 18 months of doing very little training I went to thirteen stone seven pounds. Ralph Brand took me to the side and told me that it was time to get motivated, time to start thinking about genuinely working hard, to get back to playing in the team. He made out training schedules for me, diets and everything, and we started working hard together to reduce the weight.

I can remember my first week of training morning, afternoon and night – I lost about seven pounds! Unfortunately, on the Saturday I was going to a party where the seven pounds was virtually put back on with eating and having too much to drink. On the Monday I received one of the most severe rollickings I have ever had in my football career. Ralph Brand went absolutely crazy and he was certainly not the nicest person to fall out with! He laid it on the line that if I didn't start taking everything seriously he would not waste the time and his own efforts in trying to help me get back into the first team.

About three weeks afterwards Scotland were playing England in the famous 'Auld Enemy' clash down at Wembley – the famous Stuart Kennedy 5-1 defeat. I, Ian Campbell, his brother Richard and some of our friends hired a van to take us down via Blackpool. Ralph Brand weighed me before we left and said, ''Right, you can come back at least two, possibly three, pounds heavier but any more and I am finished with you.'' So off we trekked to Blackpool, where we had a great night singing the old Scottish tunes of glory. Then on Friday we proceeded down to London with our kilts, our scarfs and our songs. Friday again was a great party night, Saturday was the game and on Sunday we came home via Blackpool again.

On Monday I was to be at training for ten a.m. We didn't arrive home until four a.m. and I phoned Ralph about nine-thirty a.m. asking him if I could have an afternoon session. When Ralph said yes, that was okay, I immediately headed for the Carnegie Baths in Dunfermline for a sauna where I stayed for an hour and a half trying to get rid off the excess water and weight that I had put on over the weekend. When I went back to East End at noon Ralph

Jim

Brand immediately weighed me and he found me to be half a pound lighter than he found me to be on the previous Friday!

Ralph couldn't believe this. He was so pleased. Hopefully, he will never find out because I'm sure the first thing he would do, especially if he found out I spent the morning in the sauna with a tracksuit and a wet-suit on, boiling and sweating pounds and pounds away, would be to come and punch me right on the gob!

Nevertheless, the truth of the matter is that I was desperate to get back as a player. Photographs at the time show me smiling and fooling around with other players in the treatment room but gradually the truth was dawning that despite all the hard work, sweating, stomach exercises, jogging and cycling, I would never be able to play to quite the same standards again. My eventual come-back in the reserve team confirmed that – I had lost a vital two yards in speed. I had been told before the injury that one day I might play for Scotland. Now I was utterly devastated.

I did play once more for the Dunfermline Athletic first team. Harry Melrose who was the manager at this time told me I was in the pool for the Clyde game on 18 February 1976. I was so excited it was like making my debut again. I prepared in every professional way and in the afternoon I went to bed for two or three hours' sleep just to make sure that I had rested fully. Going to East End on the night was terrific – the adrenalin was flowing. I was hoping and praying that I would be in the 11 named but unfortunately the team was announced and I was on the bench. No matter however, I was still in the 13 and was going to sample the atmosphere of the first team game.

The match started and Dunfermline were well on top. All through the second half, because we were on top, I had been biting Harry Melrose's ear, nagging, nagging and nagging to get a game. There was no way Dunfermline were going to get beaten, I was saying, and it was about time I got onto the pitch. He looked so fed up that with 20 minutes to go he told me to get warmed up. I was so excited that I jumped from the dugout and ran down the park. The reception was tremendous. Everyone was cheering because they hadn't seen me play for two years. I couldn't wait to get my track-suit off and get on to the pitch. But unfortunately when the time came it was such a big anti-climax – all I did for the remaining 15 minutes was take one free kick. Nevertheless it gave me fresh hope and fresh enthusiasm that one day I might be a regular in the Dunfermline Athletic team again. It was not to be.

Dunfermline did not make the Premier League and the next few years were to be bleak with the return of the yo-yo tag. I was involved next in a player-swap deal with Bobby Morrison of Cowdenbeath. It was a thrill to sign for Frank Connor, a Manager for whom I have great respect. However, as I walked around East End for the last time I felt I had made a big mistake. I only played 11 games for Cowdenbeath in the 1976-77 season but at least it was first team football. Ironically, one game was against Dunfermline at East End. The chant of "Reject, Reject" really got to me and my pal Alan Evans gave me a hard time on the pitch. In the end, in pure devilment, I pulled his shorts down! I was red carded. Was this how my career at my beloved Dunfermline was to end? The story was only beginning . . .

Chapter 4

EARLY DAYS BACK AT EAST END

Sitting, hoping to be made manager of the team
And then being told, my face was a gleam
Feeling so proud and praying for glory
Now, about the early days, I'll tell you the story

Robertson, Young and Bowie to name but a few
What a great bunch to have on your crew
McCathie and Watson, now they were two
When games got crucial, they pulled us through

Thomson, Moyes and Donnelly, what a mid-field bunch
They won every tackle when it came to the crunch
Not like Morrison – he was a fairy [only joking Stevie]
I'd have been better playing my wife, Mary
But Stevie, yer goals were some of the best I've seen
Going back to the days of the great Jock Stein!

Remember the journeys so near and so far
A cold winter's night going to Stranraer
Or poor Bobby Forrest who we had to leave
When his car got a puncture when we played against Threave

The good times, the bad times, the times of sheer passion
Old strips, the new strips, how they've changed in fashion
To all the players who played under me
Let's get together sometime and have a soirée

MONDAY, 31 October 1983, was the proudest day of my life – the day I became manager of Dunfermline Athletic Football Club. As the club's reserve coach under the recently departed Tom Forsyth I had been involved in the training that Monday evening when Mr Watters, the club chairman, asked me to stay behind for a moment. When I went through to his room he told me the incredible news. The Leishman era was under way.

How had this turn of events come around? Well, on leaving Cowdenbeath I played football for Glenrothes – in fact I was the first £100 signing in their history! From there I moved on to Oakley and had a good deal of fun but I was playing too many games, my old injury was reacting and I ended up each night with cold compresses on the swelling on my legs. I learned one important lesson in those games though, namely that there is just as much passion and commitment at this grade as there is at the top level of the game.

From Oakley I moved on to take my first steps in football management with Kelty Hearts Juniors in 1980. That period provides a fund of memories, as well as a foundation for future management techniques and disciplines. I remember one day we were playing Tulliallan at the local Juniors ground. At the time we were sitting second top of the League, trailing only by one point. We were leading 2-0 with 25 minutes to go, by which time I had used both our substitutes. However, our centre-forward, Charlie Mitchell, had been having a nightmare of a match in direct opposition to the famous ex-Celt George Connelly, Charlie had already been booked but now he started arguing with the players around him and with the referee. The ref even asked me to calm him down for his own good and I did so. Charlie's reply was, "Ach, be quiet. I'm no' gonna quieten down. I'm gettin' on wi' the game." He wasn't – I immediately removed him from the game despite having used up my substitutes.

The chairman, Ian Thompson, and his committee were frankly taken aback, especially as Kelty Hearts were challenging for the League in their very first season in the Juniors but perhaps more especially as Tulliallan proceeded to pull a goal back. But I was adamant. I had to set standards that the rest of the team could follow. No way was I going to be spoken to like any other player on the park. Anyway, Charlie Mitchell was better placed coming off there and then than being sent off and suspended for the next three or four weeks in the run in to the Championship.

After the game, which we eventually won 2-1, Charlie apologised and I accepted his apology. On the Monday the committee called

Proud to be manager: the men who gave me the job, 1983

me in front of their meeting. They made it clear that they were not pleased that I had taken such a risk but again I told them that the only real way forward for the team was to set high standards. After that no decision I made was questioned and all the players went about their business in the proper manner.

We were pipped by a point in the League that season and later there was to be a Player of the Year dance, where the trophy was to be presented. It came to my speech and I put a dampener on the occasion by declaring that being runner-up was of no interest to me. I was only interested in winning things. There were lots of whispers around the tables – a bit like *Coronation Street* gossip – but I was simply being honest about my philosophy.

I was delighted to be offered the coaching job at Cowdenbeath later that year and I learned a lot from that spell. I was really disappointed when Andy Rolland resigned as manager and, in retrospect, I made the mistake of staying on. The result was that when Hugh Wilson became the new manager he brought in his own coach and I ended up leaving without saying my farewells to the players. However, I was learning how to deal with people's feelings.

Next, on 23 July 1982, I came back to East End. It all began with a phone call from then director Martin Sisman, who invited me along to have a chat with Pat Stanton on the Monday evening. As I arrived I met Trevor Smith, who had just signed. He had been a success with the Scottish Schoolboys and a number of clubs were interested. I wished him all the best and then had a one and a half hour meeting with Pat Stanton. When I came out I was youth coach. Pat Stanton had become manager at the end of 1980-81 season and the following year the club ended up eighth equal in Division One, their best showing for more than five years. He began bringing promising players to the club, such as McCathie, Jenkins, Morrison and Forrest, but he also had permission to spend a staggering £43,000 on Aberdeen's Doug Considine. When Doug later left the club to work in a laundry the saying "being taken to the cleaners" took on a whole new meaning! Nevertheless until the Dunfermline game at home to St Johnstone there was more optimism than there had been in years. Then a vicious tackle on Jimmy Brown ended his career and the team pattern was badly affected. The club finished in a safe position but that was all.

When Hibs dispensed with their manager they invited Pat Stanton and George Stewart to take over. I was recovering from an injury in the caravan at Pettycur Bay when the news came through on the radio. I wondered about my future. Would the new man bring in his own backroom team? In the event, Tom Forsyth invited me to become the reserve coach so I'd got promotion.

When all is said and done, Tom is one of the greatest people I have ever met in the game. He has no airs and graces and gets on well with people. His main problem was that he had had a successful career with a top club and I don't think the players at East End Park were geared to the standards that Tom set. He never really adjusted from a full-time to a part-time set up.

Meanwhile I really enjoyed the period. It was great to be involved and I really had to learn how to motivate because at that level gates are tiny. I told the players that the performance was not vital but they had to be mentally aware and physically prepared to step in. Forsyth acted on my recommendations as he could only watch the reserves now and again in midweek. There were some good players in my team like Trevor Smith and Kevin Hepburn. The latter lost his way a bit but could have developed into something special.

However, the first team was in trouble and we were relegated with the highest number of points a demoted club has ever attained. Morale had not been helped by Considine walking out, while only £25,000 was taken at the turnstiles, one-sixth of what the club required. There was a last gasp fightback, including a 3-3 draw at Hearts, but to beat First Division champions St Johnstone at Muirton proved too much to ask of a struggling team.

At the start of season 1983-84, John Perry came on a free transfer from Falkirk, John Lapsley from Partick Thistle and Bobby Dall returned. A succession of poor results, including an 8-1 aggregate League Cup defeat by Dundee United, convinced Tom Forsyth, who had spent part of the period in hospital, that the time had come to give up the 80-mile trip from his home to East End. Applications were invited for the post and I believe there were 39 or 40.

I did not put in for the post but realised full well that the board would know I was never away from the ground. In any case if I applied, the new manager, whoever it was, might regard me as a threat. Of those applications I believe five were serious and Mr Watters told me the board would decide in two days. I was allowed to sign Steve Simpson, Ian Heddle and Allan Forsyth and on 22 October I made my first team selection, namely: Whyte, Crawford, Lapsley, Wilcox, Dall, Donnelly, Simpson, McCathie, Morrison, Perry, Jenkins, subs Forrest and Black. We lost 3-2 to Queen's Park.

After considering all the applications Mr Watters told me the great news. I remember saying that the wages were not important and all that mattered was that I would be in the list of managers in the club centenary history book. I was so excited that when I got home I knocked on the door of our neighbours, the Andersons and the Smarts, and we ended up having an impromptu pyjama party with coffee!

I would be the first part-time manager of Dunfermline Athletic since the war and would keep on my good post at the Job Centre. I had to take two days of my annual leave to examine the contract and check out the set up. Frankly, walking round the ground the next day for two hours was totally depressing. There was no buzz about the place at all – indeed I had three phone calls all week! It really saddened me after knowing in the late Sixties early Seventies how much buzz used to be about the place. Players mingling, players talking about the Saturday/Sunday events, players using the facilities at East End Park. Everywhere you went there were people to talk with. No more was there any of this. I felt in my heart and in my head that I had to try and achieve the glory days of the Sixties to get people talking, get people believing in the club again and get people to come and be part of it as they used to. I would have to go out looking for the media and publicity – how that would alter in the course of the next seven years!

Of full-time staff there was only Sheila Peters in the office, Danny Hutchinson on the ground staff and Sandy, the "boots boy". It was an awful anti-climax. Something had to be done. There had been so much talk about the "Sleeping Giant" but, no matter how much it was prodded, it continued in its slumbers.

Anyway, my first win came on 5 November, when a Steve Morrison goal got us the points at Montrose. I wrote in the programme that there was no one more keen than I to bring back the halcyon days to the club but in the next two months we only had that one win, and to add to the depression the home fans were briefly deprived of their programme!

I knew the players I had inherited were just not capable of mounting a realistic league challenge. I would have to bring in new players. One of them, at the end of 1983, was called John Watson.

It became more and more clear that I faced a stiff uphill struggle. The club only had three sets of strips and Joe Nelson performed miracles with the training gear, such as it was. But I began to concentrate on building up the team spirit and did this initially by having the players on nights out together. I also had to build up the loyalty of my part-time backroom staff of Pip Yeates, Joe Nelson and Andy Young. Within three weeks I had gained their respect but not in the sort of circumstances I would have desired. Before a match I would often give the players final instructions on the pitch. Some had a long warm-up but often others waited in the dressing-room. One day a director had gone into the dressing-room and spoken to the players. I learned this from the backroom staff and went straight to the board where I made it plain I would resign rather than countenance any interference. I was backed 100 per cent by Mr Watters but the other director did not speak to me for a month. From then on I had a great relationship with the board too!

Only the diehards supported the club and crowds were numbered in their hundreds. There was a big world out there – I would have to "manage the town". Part of that entailed getting the kiosks in local superstores to sell the DAFC raffle tickets again and going to any social nights or charity events that would invite me.

On the playing front that season there are two games I instantly recall. There is nothing better than a Cup game to lift depression and we were due to meet Forfar, who were going well at the top of the division. We simply had nothing to lose and we put them out in a superb game with Rab Stewart's goal taking us to a plum tie at Ibrox. We gave the Rangers scouts the best of treatment when they came to watch us that evening but when we sent people to spy on them I remember we had to buy the tickets! I used that slight later in my team talk.

About six or seven inches of snow fell that week but the game was bound to be on due to the undersoil heating. On Tuesday evening we trained with a rugby ball on our frosty park and on the Thursday we had relay races at Carnegie Baths! In contrast Rangers jetted off to prepare in Majorca. We had one problem – Lapsley was injured – so I played Bobby Forrest at full-back and it was a success. On the day of the big game I briefed the lads fully in the morning. I would play McCathie in front of the back four and Donnelly was to pick up Russell.

We had lunch at the Burnbrae Hotel, then the coach got lost for a while and we arrived at the stadium at ten minutes past two. I began to talk individually to each player. Suddenly I realised that Steve Morrison was wearing a black suit and matching tie. I grabbed the tie and choked him. "You're not here for a funeral," I told him. "If you are dead now, how will you be at three o'clock?" He went on to win the Scottish Health and Education "Mr Superfit" award so we threatened to choke him more often after that!

That game has become history now – indeed in a sense it was the day we began on the long road back. Mao said a journey of 1,000 miles starts with a single step – well, we took ours that day. It was a magnificent performance and we came within nine minutes of a far greater turn up than the infamous result at Berwick in 1967. Our team was Whyte, Dall, Forrest, Wilcox, Forsyth, Donnelly, Smith, McCathie, Stewart, Morrison, Tait, substitutes Watson and Hepburn. We absorbed massive pressure then began to find our feet. Donnelly did a good job on play-maker Russell and then we began to play some attractive football before an 18,000 crowd, almost equal to our entire league gate. Suddenly, in the 59th minute, Donnelly disposessed McClelland, found Rab Stewart in acres of space on the left and he calmly rounded Nicky Walker and shot home, the ball taking a slight deflection off McAdam.

Suddenly there were scenes of great joy especially in our dugout. Before the game we only had so many tickets, two for each player. Because of such high demand for tickets the players and staff, myself and anyone connected with the background staff were looking for three or four tickets each. Unfortunately Rangers couldn't give us any more or wouldn't give us any more. What we did then was decide to try and cram as many people in the dugout as we possibly could. Eventually there must have been ten people in the dugout which normally held six. This caused a problem when we scored the goal as everyone in the dugout was jumping, screaming, shouting and everyone was banging their heads, elbows and their knees and hitting against each other.

I jumped out on the park to get some breathing space. I was so excited I was trying to shout to the players to tell them to try and not lose a quick goal because Rangers would respond with a vengeance. I don't think the players heard me because of the volume of noise that was coming from the terracing – not to mention the dugout.

As the game continued my heart stopped as McCoist and McClelland had goals disallowed and Clark could do nothing right. We felt that McAdam should have been sent off but in the 81st minute, as the fates would have it, he pushed up front and headed the equaliser. With legs giving out in the Pars defence, Ally McCoist got the winner in the 83rd minute.

Our performance in that match had totally belied our lowly position. Some of my players wept in the dressing-room afterwards. They were shattered and some could hardly stand. I had run up on to the pitch and shaken each player's hand and big Jock Wallace told me our tactics had been absolutely right. He had been worried – whatever he told the papers afterwards! I had worn my camel coat that day and the person in football I would most like to meet is the person who stole it a few months later!

The following month there was an equally significant moment when Gregor Abel became coach. His first game saw our first home victory in over three months! Inconsistent form and three defeats in our last four games meant we had ended up in our worst position in 30 years – ninth in Division Two. I didn't have the money of my predecessors to spend but new players would have to be brought in. Meanwhile Director Martin Sisman begged the *Dunfermline Press* not to stress how low we had finished!

At the start of 1984-85 only one thing was on my mind and that was the aim of gaining promotion in our centenary year. Rab Stewart went to Motherwell for £10,000 and I signed Rowan Hamilton from Dundee, and Paul Rodgers from Happy Valley, Hong Kong, and Dave Young from Arbroath. A goal machine was taking shape. A fit, lean John Watson scored four in the 5-0 romp against Stranraer; a resounding 4-0 Skol Cup victory over Arbroath gave us a lucrative tie with Celtic; and by the time that was played, we had gone top of the League, beating Raith 3-1 away.

You would have thought the halcyon days had already returned the night we played Celtic. I knew the boys would need no motivating but I would have to psyche them up for a game where all the media had written us off. As we sat in the dressing-room I wrote the Celtic names on the blackboard and then rubbed their names off in turn, saying crazy things like, "Look you are playing Willie McStay – aren't you glad it's not Paul?" . . . "Reid will be attacking so that will leave gaps at the back which we can exploit" . . . "Burns is out of position" . . . "McAdam will have to use his wrong foot" . . . and so on! Then, as they left, I said, ludicrously, "Really you are only playing seven men!"

When John Watson scored a fabulous goal in the first half, I jumped out of the dugout and even Joe Nelson could not restrain me. Suddenly a burly police sergeant said, "If you don't get back in that dugout you'll hear the rest of the game on my walkie talkie!" I kept roaring out lots of instructions until John Watson shouted back at me to calm down. So much for my concern that the players would not be able to handle the situation!

Celtic had us under relentless pressure after the half-time cuppa and I thought the roof might fall in when they hit two in three minutes, but back came John to score again. I felt that only their superior fitness eventually gave them the game with no need for extra time.

By the time we had won the opening six games I commented that I could not remember the club having made a better start to a season. As I explain elsewhere, the 1-0 defeat at Ochilview was very disappointing, although we recovered to take ten points from the next six games and 4,300 watched the home game with Alloa. After that we entered an erratic period which in retrospect would cost us promotion and which culminated in perhaps my worst result as Dunfermline's manager. It had been bad enough to lose 2-0 in lashing rain at Firs Park but that December we lost 3-1 to East Stirling in the Cup and the statisticians reminded me we had not fared so badly since 1953!

January and February provided no let up in the sequence of bad results, starting with a 2-1 home derby by Raith. I signed Lidell and O'Connor but neither proved as successful as I'd hoped. Like George Miller before me, I had to sign the best players I could get my hands on in the free transfer circuit and sometimes I got it wrong. That was to be the case with Colin McGlashan, whom I could not fit in up front with Watson and Jenkins who were such good partners, but Colin's later career proved what a competent player he was. By March, Perry, O'Connor and Lidell had departed. We were now so well adrift of Alloa and Montrose that all hope seemed gone.

The club needed money to buy quality players and I was delighted when I was approached to take on the added role of commercial manager full-time. I had been going out to the supporters, meeting them at their own venues – their supporters' clubs, their pubs, their social clubs and trying to encourage them to come to East End more. I also went to the youth clubs, boys clubs and schools. Mr Watters saw me as a terrific salesman for Dunfermline Football Club.

I paused for ten to 15 minutes to think about giving up the security of being a civil servant with the Employment Services Division at Cowdenbeath Job Centre. But again my love for the club was to overrule all other thoughts in my head. I was delighted to accept and I have never regretted for one moment taking the commercial job. It involved organising the lottery side and ticket sales along with Jessie Arnott, who was a tremendous help. The job also involved trying to find new ventures such as the Centenary Club. We persuaded the board to go into the venture. It is a great organisation and gets the fans together on several occasions for social nights, functions or golf outings. It has also been proved to be financially rewarding for Dunfermline Athletic Football Club.

Anyway, by the time we went to Alloa in midweek only a win was going to do. Jimmy Thompson, their manager, said that if Alloa won, it was all over. Nothing I could have said could have irritated the players more. The evening before I had watched a McGuigan fight on TV and I told the players they had to match that same commitment and hammer their opponents. A large travelling support saw a great performance and we ran out 3-1 winners.

Then a 2-1 home defeat to Cowdenbeath wiped out all the good work. We were doing well away from home but a home win against East Stirling in March was the first in five months. By the time we defeated Stranraer away I had brought in David Moyes, Ian Westwater and Ian Campbell. I had the nucleus of a strong team and some erratic results by Alloa kept hopes alive that we could still do it in our special year. The problem was that every time we got into a challenging position we let ourselves down. Raith defeated Alloa but we could only draw with East Stirling and Albion Rovers. A 0-0 draw with leaders Montrose did not help the cause, but when Alloa had another shock defeat we blew it by losing 2-3 in a cracker of a game with Raith, who were on a magnificent run. We defeated Queen of the South 4-0 which meant that going into our last two games we were one point adrift of Alloa who had a goal difference of $+17$ to our $+24$. The next game would be at Alloa!

Some have said that we didn't really want promotion but the 4,000-plus Pars fans who packed into little Recreation Park that sunny afternoon know how disappointed we were with the 0-0 scoreline. In the 71st minute, a handball gave us a penalty but Stevie Morrison struck it weakly and under enormous pressure it was saved. Nine times out of ten Stevie would have scored, but let me put on record that, if I could go back to that moment in the Tardis, I would still ask him to take the spot kick.

What happened next was the cruellest moment one can have in a game. All we could do was defeat lowly Berwick and hope that miraculously, bottom team Arbroath could draw with Alloa. In a changing game we were drawing 1-1 at half time and knew Alloa were 1-0 up. We missed chance after chance until Trevor Smith coolly slammed his second penalty of the afternoon into the corner of the net, with the ball causing a small sandstorm as it landed on the baked pitch. As the game was played out a rumour began on the far terracing, based on a radio report, that Arbroath had equalised and it spread like wild fire. As the whistle went the players were mobbed by the fans in their ecstasy and the celebrations began. But suddenly the joy in the dressing-room and the mutual congratulations were extinguished as a policeman came to the door and told us quietly that Alloa had won! I felt I had to go out to the fans, who were expecting victory speeches and, choking back the tears, I told them the news. I remember the fans dispersed noiselessly and all went quiet in the dressing-room.

The determination of the following season was born in that moment. I made the remark later that it was like winning the pools only to learn the coupon had not been posted. Only Motherwell outwith the Premier League had been better supported.

★ ★ ★

The summer and autumn of 1985 are obviously remembered for all the wonderful centenary celebrations. The highlight, naturally, was the centenary match against Aberdeen on 7 August, when all the hard work of the office staff in bringing back former players was rewarded. Some of them really were old-timers. Among them were Alex Edwards, Jackie Sinclair, Willie Callaghan, Jim Fraser, Charlie Dickson, Bert Paton, Paddy Wilson, Pat Gardner, Alex Totten, Alex Ferguson, George Miller, Alex Wright, Alan Evans, Harry Melrose, Alex Smith, Jimmy Cannon, Gerry Mays, Barrie Mitchell, Walter Borthwick, Jim Thomson and Mike Leonard. Some of these assembled stars had gone on to greater things yet they had all retained a great affection for the club and felt it had been

Courtesy of Dunfermline Athletic Football Club

Victory celebrations

71

a vital part of their lives. We laid on a free bar for them in the gym and it was a great night out. As you supped your beer you could watch the video of all the great games of the 1960s. The star of the evening was Jock Stein and everyone wanted to speak to the big man. He was not just a hero for Dunfermline Athletic but to any Scots fan and his achievements of nine League wins, a European Cup and managing Scotland, speak volumes for him.

Jock had always been my hero. As a young lad I had stood outside to get his autograph and when he came out in the rain I offered him a scrap of paper. As he fiddled for a pen he said in that distinctive gruff voice, "Don't you have an autograph book, lad?"

I recall I met him as a player when we lost 2-6 to Celtic in a Drybrough Cup-tie. I managed to score an own goal which helped Celtic's cause and which was to encourage my Celtic-supporting brother to goad me with the statistic that I was their top goalscorer along with Hood and Lennox, it being the start of the season. Well, Jock came in to speak to us and said, "Look the result is not important, all you have do to this season is stay up!" Strangely, our next game in the League was against them again and we only lost 2-3. It was unusual that he should spare a word to help us but that was so typical of the man. He will always have a special place in my affections. At any rate the evening was a big success helped by the fact that we defeated Aberdeen 1-0.

Around this time a Pars fan ran a meeting at the Old Inn at the Kirkgate, where the club had been formed 100 years earlier. Then, with the advice of Nat Lofthouse, the "Centenary Club" was formed. Bolton had been in dire straits but the commercial venture had saved them and I learned of the scheme at a meeting of Commercial Managers in Dunblane. It has been a huge success and so far has brought in £150,000 for the club while giving the fans fabulous prizes, discounts in local shops, precedence for ticket sales and a chance to come together in a variety of social outings ranging from snooker and golf to *Cats* and pantos! There was a Centenary Dinner at the same venue in August with Bob Crampsey as Master of Ceremonies and the 300 guests had a great evening of entertainment. Bob, author of *Mr Stein* and Scotland's top sports analysist, also introduced the clips on the Dunfermline video. Almost every football club in Scotland attended the club's official centenary dinner at Crossford in November too. Finally Bob Crampsey chaired the wonderful "Audience with Jock Stein" at the Carnegie

Hall. Jock took a great interest in the celebrations and made a few visits after that, including one to the local museum displaying Pars memorabilia. The museum has never known such interest before or since!

On the playing side I was confident of promotion with the squad who had come so close last time out but I brought in Houston from Alloa, Roddy Grant and Willie Callaghan, a name older Pars fans knew well. We drew 3-3 at Arbroath where we had been tipped to win, but I still wrote in the programme that "in the dressing-room there is an atmosphere I have never seen at the club before, except in the 1960s when I came as a teenage player. There was a determination to win among the lads, not only for themselves but also for the fans who have given such tremendous support throughout the years." In the event, the Skol Cup game against Stenhousemuir was off due to torrential rain. It had been the wettest summer in years and East End had yet to get the sand slitting which would remedy the annual problem. We eventually won that match 4-0.

We took three points from the first three league games and we had lost 3-1 to Queens Park, a certain Ian McCall doing the damage by scoring twice. Our determination was in evidence when we defeated Cowdenbeath 3-2 despite being two goals down at one point and then drawing 3-3 in a cracker at home to Raith. That match was preceded by the minute's silence for Jock Stein who had died suddenly in the World Cup qualifying game in Cardiff.

I was delighted when there was a Testimonial Match for Jim Bowie, Hugh Whyte, Paul Donelly and Bobby Robertson because I felt they had given so much to the club without a great deal of reward.

By October we had gone nine games without a defeat and our biggest win of the season, 6-0 against Albion Rovers, prompts a memory. We were 3-0 up in that game even by half time so I said to Gregor, "If we score early in the second half it will be all over and I'll go and sit in the stand." Well, we did score and I kept hearing Mr Watters in the directors box muttering, "This is not good enough, we aren't fit enough" and the like. When we scored the fifth and the sixth I was convinced that would stop him – but he kept it up! He even complained after the game about our performance, yet when we lost 2-3 to Stirling, a game in which we had a magnificent fightback, he had praised us to the hilt!

We were fairly rattling in the goals in that period and it was no

73

wonder that the fans called Stevie Morrison "Zico" after the swerving free kick against Meadowbank at home which gave us a 1-1 draw. We won every league game in November and gates were topping 4,000.

That month took in the famous incident against Queen of the South whom we defeated 2-1. The scoreline may now be forgotten but many a fan will recall the moment when Jimmy Bowie, who was having a blinder, beat Tony Gervaise easily and Gervaise then collapsed. "Ziggy" had got to the byeline and was in a dangerous position but suddenly left the ball and called the ref over to stop the play. We did not realise what had occurred and were roaring in annoyance at him but it turned out that on that bitterly cold day Tony had hypothermia and had to be rushed off for treatment.

The 2-0 win before Christmas against Raith Rovers was a relief – Bobby Wilson's team had just defeated Stenhousemuir 9-2! I think everyone knows the story that we beat Raith in the Cup after a joke-telling session in the dressing-room but not so well known were the events surrounding the crazy Cup day at non-league Threave. It was my first meeting with referee Louis Thow since an infamous day at Ochilview but he was to have a good game and, to his credit, did not bear a grudge. It was Threave's biggest game in their history and our few fans had travelled a huge distance to get there. The snow fell heavily and that journey was on Thow's mind as he considered whether it was advisable even to make a start. The committee asked that I speak to the fans, because 1,600 were crammed into a ground that usually held 200 and most of them were trying to survive the elements under cover in a "Cowshed" while the directors tried to keep warm in the team coach and did not venture out. I was asked to sing *EastEnders* but drew the line at that. I was more concerned about where Bobby Forrest had got to, even though I knew we had Ian Heddle as cover. We had missed Bobby at the Maybury and Hamilton pick up points and that was totally out of character. In the event he turned up in an Edinburgh cab with £70 on the meter! Jimmy McConville quickly wrote a cheque for £7. The look on his face when the taxi driver told him the real fare was a picture. "That's your bonus gone," he told Bobby. When I saw one of the Threave boys warming up in golf shoes I did wonder how I was going to motivate the lads! Well, we won 5-0 comfortably but the journey back in the coach on a freezing cold day was horrendous after a

The real Mr Dunfermline, J. McConville

snowball with a large stone inside went through the back window in Dumfries.

Two league wins in January set us up for the seemingly inevitable Cup-tie at Hibs. Alex Ferguson surprised many by calling it "the tie of the round" but we could think back to our centenary game victory over Aberdeen in August and we were confident, with Hibs being near the foot of the table. We took 5,000 fans to the capital and the 13,500 crowd was Hibs' biggest so far that season. Being part-time we knew it would not be easy against a team with the goalkeeping experience of Rough, a strike force of the prolific Durie and Cowan and the class of Collins and Kane. I felt we were doing well to frustrate them but the harsh sending off of Moyes changed the game and the 2-0 defeat was not a disgrace.

By defeating East Stirling 2-1 we had beaten the record of going 17 consecutive league games without defeat, a run that ended in the 2-3 defeat at the hands of Stirling Albion. A late goal by Irvine ruined a classic fightback with goals by Young and Smith in the dying minutes.

The harsh winter led to more postponements and February 1986 will be remembered for the *Pebble Mill* adventure and the suggestion that Dunfermline Athletic should become a member of a breakaway league. At first I felt that would be great but I was having a drink one evening with former Pars and Raith player, Paddy Wilson, who argued that while it would be good to go full-time again and instantly see the return of big crowds, wouldn't it be all the more pleasurable and credible to achieve all that on our own merits? I, for one, do not really want to see a Super League which would mean an end to the Cowdenbeaths, East Stirlings and Stenhousemuirs. However, I do see the case of the likes of Inverness and East Kilbride being admitted to the League and maybe the solution is to relocate teams, with, for example, Clyde moving to a new town. While it would work to have Hearts and Hibs in a superstadium in the capital I do not think Clyde and Partick sharing Firhill has been a great success.

Well, we were now second in the table, one point behind Queen of the South but well clear of third-placed St Johnstone, while my utter commitment to the cause is best exemplified by the 4-4 result at Berwick where we were 4-1 down but came back to equalise. We each had a player sent off and Manager Eric Tait and I almost came to blows on the track. I had taken my jacket off and said, "I will settle this here and now", but Joe Nelson pulled me back and ripped the arms of my jacket in the process!

In March we won four games and drew four, the overtime being created by all the postponed games. Queen's Park were catching us up but this was due to their undersoil heating – they had played three games more. Promotion was starting to look assured. At Meadowbank we drew 2-2 when an Ian Campbell "goal" appeared to have crossed the line – but the ref waved play on denying us victory! After the vital 3-0 away win against Albion Rovers I snapped up the versatile Gary Thompson from Alloa, whose aggression and commitment I felt would be a huge benefit to us.

Suddenly we stuttered wtih 1-3 and 0-4 defeats at Queen of the South and Meadowbank. Because of injuries and call-offs we ended up with Hamish McAlpine in goals in the latter game! Hugh Whyte was on holiday and Ian Westwater had phoned to say he had been in bed and was not fit to play. I think I phoned every club in Scotland and even tried for Peter McCloy, but in the end Jim McLean said I could use Hamish McAlpine although he warned

In good voice

Eat your heart out Phil Collins: myself, Billy Rankin, Greg Abel and Dan McCafferty presenting the gold disc for the EastEnders record

that he had a bad knee. I went up to Tannadice, got him signed, zoomed back to Glasgow to get him registered and at eight at night, kick-off time, he was in the team. I felt his ability to throw the ball accurately would make up for the fact he couldn't kick that evening. We were soon 2-0 down and it turned into a rout. It was the worst defeat of the season and had come at a bad time. Hamish and I can laugh about it now, but I had a clear-the-air meeting with the players to discuss the two bad results and suffice to say we won the next five games on the trot, four of them by 4-0 and the other by 2-0, and they included the great night against St Johnstone when John Watson took his total goal tally for the season to 30 and won the Golden Shot award and champagne.

When we defeated East Stirling 2-0 we knew that if Cowdenbeath could draw at Hampden then we were up – and this time there was no mistake in the news that Cowdenbeath had won! East End went wild with fans swamping the players and as we celebrated in the dressing-room we savoured the fact that we had achieved it with four games to spare. Queen of the South were also promoted but they were one point clear. That changed after we defeated Arbroath 2-0 on a day when Queen of the South lost to Stirling. Then when we beat Berwick 4-0, with Queen of the South losing again, we became champions elect.

On 29 April, two days later, after the dinner dance celebrating the 1961 Cup win and featuring the team that day, we were to meet Stenhousemuir while Queen of the South were playing at Central Park. If we won, the title was ours for the first time in 60 years but if we drew they would have to draw as well.

Prior to the game, with Gregor and me doing all we could to handle the pressure and with a big crowd packed into the small ground, a guy ran up to us and said "That's all my pies sold already." There was half an hour till kick-off time! Westy kept us in the game early on with two fine saves but there were groans when we learned that Queen of the South were 3-1 up. I kept shouting to the lads to keep it tight, make no mistakes, hold on, but it seemed it would not be the championship evening after all. The whistle went, the players shook hands and the fans made their way to the exits. The announcer was giving out some trivia over the tannoy when suddenly he said, "I have a score here that may be of interest. It's Cowdenbeath 3 Queen of the South 3.

The little park just erupted. I ended up along with John Watson

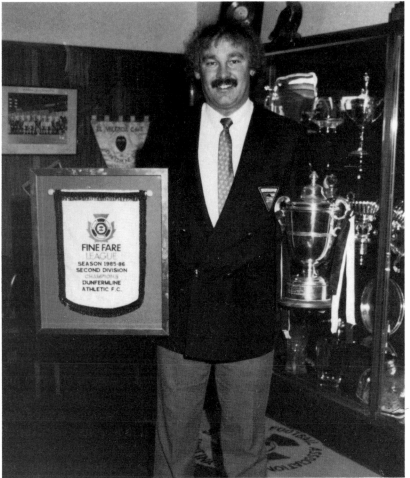

Courtesy of Dunfermline Athletic Football Club

Second Division Champions, 1986

on supporters' shoulders. All the fans joined in the celebrations and the champagne corks popped in the dressing-room. There was singing and dancing and it crossed my mind that it was ironic that Cowdenbeath, who had so much to lose with us going up, should be the team to do it for us! I always remember too the seconds of disbelief as the fans took the scoreline in.

All the way back to Dunfermline horns were hooted as the happy convoy made its way back. First we went back to celebrate at the Paragon and it was a nice touch when the disappointed Queen of the South team joined us, to congratulate us. Nobby Clark and I

Former Pars Chairman, Jim Watters (we did it for you)

discussed the season over a few drinks. No wonder a few days later
the fans bought 1,500 strips in three hours!

We eventually ended up at the East Port Bar and during the fantastic celebrations John Watson came over and asked for a loan to
buy a drink. I said I had no cash on me but to go and get a few
drinks. The following day I got a bill for £175 at my home. He had

told the bar staff the drinks were on me! Later I realised that Norrie was posted missing and he turned up in the rafters where he had gone for some peace and quiet!

The following Saturday we lost 2-3 at Stirling and maybe the effects of all that champagne had got to us. Bobby Robertson was presented with the Second Division Championship Trophy the following day. I have never seen a prouder man. It wasn't just the football club that had been revived, it was the whole town.

Chapter 5

UPS AND DOWNS
Promotion 1986-87

Promotion, relegation, the football ups and downs
Bring smiles and laughter or tears and frowns
I've sampled them both during my management career
But nothing can beat a promotion year
Relegation it takes you to the depths of despair
Three teams going down to me wasn't fair
At the start of the season team chances are the same
But in the Premier League it's a different ball game
Some teams aim to make the top five
The others only hope to survive
The one place to be is in the top ten
I'm really glad the Pars are back there again

AS the new season began I told the media that I would be happy to consolidate this year; I was not going to get involved in promising miracles but I was sure we would cause a few upsets and would let other teams know just who we were. In reality I felt we had a chance of promotion. I saw the main threat coming from recently relegated Morton and Dumbarton, and Airdrie, who of course had Premier experience.

In seven years as manager I didn't once lose the first game of the season. That was important because if you get a good start then you have a good platform, there are no thoughts of relegation and it takes all the pressure off. It was going to be a hard season because with all the talks of league reconstruction no Premier teams had been relegated. Our Division numbered 12 clubs and that meant four games against each other. However, although it would be a difficult season, I felt this would work to our advantage.

I had retained 19 players and now I signed Eric Ferguson, Grant Reid and Ian McCall. We preferred Eric to Brian McNaughton who later moved to East Fife. Eric, we knew, was top scorer with Rangers Reserves and had been a pupil at Dunfermline High. Unsettled at Ibrox, he had been farmed out to play for Clydebank and when Graeme Souness became Rangers manager, he was given a free transfer and we simply snapped him up. He had to be persuaded because a host of other clubs were after him but we had the best wages in the Division and considerable potential. We were also the best supported club outwith the Premier Division with 10,000 more watching us than Division One champions Hamilton in 1985-86! Grant Reid had been a magnificent defender with Stenhousemuir while Ian McCall, with his skilful left foot and ability to take on defenders, had been a thorn in our flesh whenever we met Queen's Park.

With such a large squad I felt we should "go for it". Two teams would gain promotion and we would sustain a challenge because we were better equipped than most to do so.

While hard training progressed in Pettycur Bay, where my family has a caravan, and Portobello, things were happening off the pitch too. Mr Rennie, who had been responsible for the building of the Paragon Social Club, became the new chairman and one of the first tasks was to ensure that East End had a few modifications carried out in line with the Popplewell enquiry. Under the stand the Jock Stein Lounge was created by art teacher Ken Forbes. After Mr Stein's tragic death the directors felt that they should commemorate the outstanding job he had done for the club in both the Cup and in Europe. Today it is a players' lounge, a place where they can entertain guests after a game. The green carpet has all the football pitch markings, while the main focus is on big Jock leaping out of the dugout as the whistle goes in the 1961 Cup final replay – and that is all three-dimensional!

After the usual Fife Cup game we had a creditable 2-2 draw in a friendly with Aberdeen. On 9 August the new season began and the Forfar players clapped the lads on to the pitch. It was a proud moment for the people of the town and for everyone connected with the club when the Second Division flag was unfurled for the first time in 60 years. I was especially proud to be only the second

83

Dunfermline manager to achieve this. The flag was to fly proudly on the roof of the stand till one September night it was stolen! Once recovered it would only be flown on match days.

I knew that a Premier Division place was not impossible and said as much in the programme. Forfar were a formidable side who had come close to promotion themselves, but the larger than normal crowd helped gear our players up in a hectic and exciting game. A controversial John Watson goal gave us a vital 1-0 win and we were off and running. When we defeated the favourites Morton and Dumbarton 1-0 in consecutive games I knew my comments were justified. We were already top of the League and I was really confident about the Skol Cup-tie with St Mirren.

It was to be my worst Cup disappointment apart from that East Stirling game! St Mirren were an experienced team with the likes of Dougie Bell and Frank McGarvey but they had made a poor start to the season and would be without Tony Fitzpatrick. There was a good crowd of more than 6,000, the press tipped us to win, and we had the chances but lost bad goals and captain Bobby Robertson into the bargain.

A win against Clyde had us on eight points from four games by the time we were to meet Dave Clarke's East Fife. Again everyone tipped us to win. They had done little in the League and I reckoned they would be exhausted after doing so well against Rangers in midweek. In the event East Fife played out of their skins and won 2-4. At one point 0-4 down, we put up a magnificent fightback but it was too big a leeway even with Ian Campbell almost scoring at the death! One of my regrets is that I have never beaten my old foe Dave Clarke there or at Falkirk although there were a few draws. (So, Dave, the sooner you and I get back in the game the better, mate!)

Again there were important goings-on off the park. I had the players kitted out in blazers and flannels which gave the club a good image and encouraged group identity. I became the full-time manager and gave up the commercial side, which was taken up by Australian Karen Grega. Since August we'd had a team of youngsters full-time on the YTS scheme but by October things were looking promising and those players, mainly the younger ones who were not on big wages at the time, elected to go full-time. Going part-time I always felt had hastened the club's decline – now it would be that much easier attracting the better players. I was not so proud of the fact that the SFA had banned me to the stand where my walkie-talkie became indispensable.

Well, we took 18 points from the first 11 games, i.e. the first quarter, and it set us up nicely for the remainder of the season. Games against Kilmarnock always bring back memories of classic encounters in the 1960s when we were the top provincial teams, but our 2-1 win there that September stirs two particularly vivid memories. It was one of those occasions when being reduced to ten men after a sending off seemed to inspire us and we were treated to a wonderful goal by Bobby Forrest who took a pass from the halfway line from Ian McCall, strode down the left, ran into the box and let go a rocket that gave McCulloch no chance. Meanwhile our new youth team was up in Inverness taking part in a top youth tournament. They played really well and knocked out a good German team before losing in the final. I screamed back to East End from Kilmarnock, picked up three players and raced north, as I knew that trophies were being handed out at a reception and I was meant to be there with Bobby Wilson and chief scout Sandy Brown. I arrived so late they had just finished their meal and were preparing for speeches as I dashed in. At the top table I saw the German team with a person they called the "burgermeister". This roly-poly figure looked the spitting image of that same character in *William Tell*. He stood up with his interpreter and I saw Bobby Murdoch and Jimmy Johnstone beckoning me to join them. Suddenly Jinky shouted out, "What about your wig?" Of course everyone, including the German, glared at me and I could only shrug at Bobby Wilson and deny it was me!

The new full-time set up was not ideal but it was a start and we still trained the part-timers on Tuesday and Thursday evenings. A 4-1 win at Brechin was typical of that season's good results away, then we defeated Partick and Montrose at home and drew 0-0 with Airdrie, with whom we were neck and neck, on a day when the opposition repeatedly hit woodwork and "Westy" had a wonder save from Frye. A host of clubs were watching the lads by now but I had no intention of selling. As I explain elsewhere in the book, the fans witnessed a cracking 3-3 draw at Forfar where they will recall the diving header by Norrie McCathie which gave us a share of the points. Grant Reid broke his nose and Davie Young, out to show me what he could do, replaced him. Eric Ferguson had not been playing well and I had him on the bench that day. At 2-1 down

I had him warning up but Donnelly, who was having a blinder, set up a Watson goal and I decided to keep the same formation. Eric was very unhappy and apparently phoned a director later to complain. The director told him it was not his concern and referred him to me. We never had the same relationship again after that.

We only took 11 points from the next quarter. We had become the team to beat and crowds were on the way up, hence the disappointment of a 0-1 defeat by Dumbarton when we had been three points clear. However, wins against Brechin, Partick and Kilmarnock maintained that advantage. By the time of yet another defeat 2-1 by East Fife I could not help but be aware of the speculation linking me first with the manager's job at Aberdeen and then at Hibernian. However I had no intention of leaving, I had my new contract and I was determined to get the club into the Premier Division. Nor was it true that Gregor was to go to Aberdeen as assistant manager.

The worst defeat of the whole season came in late November when we lost 3-0 at Broomfield. "Westy" was injured and against a strong wind it had proved hard to clear our lines. Fortunately our main opponents were also dropping points and we still led at the halfway stage, one point clear of Dumbarton and four from Morton. One of the most important games would be in mid-December against Dumbarton at Boghead. We adopted an "up and at them" approach from the start and did not allow them to settle. Dumbarton did not appear to match our team spirit that day and we were encouraged by an early McCall strike. They equalised but yet again Norrie McCathie popped up in the dying minutes to nod home a late winner. It was only Dumbarton's second home defeat and John Wood of Radio Forth, with his tongue very firmly in his cheek, dubbed it the "Clash of the Titans"! I still feel that Dunfermline are never under the same pressure playing away from home and I firmly believed that the presence that day of a 4,000-plus crowd had given all the players great encouragement. I was delighted when, in Christmas week, Norrie repeated the dose to give us a vital 2-2 draw at Morton.

Suddenly, though, there was a new problem. I was aware that a number of top clubs were having us watched. Gordon McQueen of Airdrie rated our John Watson highly and had recommended him to Crystal Palace's Steve Coppell, who came up twice to watch John. I must admit it did cross my mind at the time that McQueen's

Dunfermline Youth team

Courtesy of Dunfermline Athletic Football Club

Exhausted but victorious after the win against Dundee in the BP Youth Cup
final, 4 May 1988

Airdrie were one of our main challengers in the First Division! Anyway, Crystal Palace came in with a £75,000 bid. The board decided that there was no way we were going to part with someone as crucial to our promotion challenge as John and the bid was turned down.

This was to lead to the first real argument between Big John and myself. John was very disappointed that I had not kept him up to date with the Crystal Palace enquiry. He had read something in the newspaper and came into my office really annoyed, demanding to know why he had not been kept in touch. Obviously he was disappointed as the prospect of full-time English football and bigger wages had a natural appeal. I told John that there was nothing concrete from the Crystal Palace side but really in my heart I knew I didn't want to lose him as he was such an important part of the team. What I did realise at that time, though, was to make sure that in future any player involved in transfer speculation had to be kept notified. It was in his interests as well as those of Dunfermline Athletic Football Club. It was the player's career and the player's livelihood and if it was for the best for both parties, then I would in future always make sure a deal could be reached. I don't think John ever forgave me for that but I learned a lesson I will never forget. To John's eternal credit, he did not let the matter interfere with his game at all. There really was such a great team spirit at that time and he was aware that his wish would come true if we got promotion. I just had to hold my breath every time there seemed to be a job for him on an oil rig!

It had been agreed that work should start on building the new turnstiles at the ground while the club was honoured when John Watson and Norrie McCathie were chosen for the Scotland semi-professional squad. Ian Campbell became assistant coach to Gregor, helping mainly with the reserves.

No supporter at the New Year game that season will easily forget it. At three o'clock we agreed with the referee that the pitch was playable but on a bitterly cold day, down came the driving snow. It became a mud bath and there were several inches of water. John Donnelly, despite the lads wearing two strips, went off with hypothermia, umpteen players were booked and Grant Jenkins not only got his 50th Pars goal but managed to score at both ends! After the 2-2 game versus Kilmarnock the winter weather meant no more games for almost a month.

The video of the club's exploits in the 1960s came out and it was titled *DAFC – The Golden Years*. It had all the top Cup and European games from the STV archives and the introductions were done by Bob Crampsey in his usual expert way, though our success on the pitch suggested that the fans were discussing that period less often now. The new "Pars Pounds" began, with kiosks in Asda, Finefare and the Kingsgate and they brought in much needed revenue.

The video had shown the great 1965 Cup semi-final win exploits against Hibs and, for the fifth time in just 12 seasons, we were drawn to meet them again. We were full of confidence as the Edinburgh side were not having a good season. About 6,000 fans were in evidence at our end of the stadium and I felt that after this game our away support began to firm up. A lot of fans who perhaps did not come regularly had come to that one and liked what they had seen. There had to be a poem: "Oh Lord I'll tell ye ne mair fibs, if ye'll only let me beat the Hibs!" Undersoil heating defeated the weather and there was the irony that Alex Miller, who had engineered our defeat by St Mirren back in August, had now replaced John Blackley at Easter Road. We had prepared all week for the game and gave a good account of ourselves but Mickey Weir's goal on the half-time whistle came at a bad time. We pressed forward for long stages but Rough had us all in despair with great saves from Young and Watson in particular. A poor Forrest pass-back let Kane in and the game was theirs.

I felt that we were at least three of four players short of a team that could maintain a place at the highest level. It is difficult to lead from the front but after wins over Clyde and Partick I joked. "It is boring when you keep on winning – you cannot slag anyone!" Against Partick they scored virtue of a John Donnelly own goal which made up, I suppose, for the day when he scored for us in a Partick jersey! I'm sure that is some sort of record.

Despite a bad defeat at Forfar we had 43 points at the three-quarter mark and were three clear of Morton, four from Dumbarton. We were all saddened at this time by the death of Jock Thompson, Kenny's Dad, who had done so much for our training under George Miller and Harry Melrose and had helped athletes with their sprinting. He was a super person.

We were delighted to beat Dumbarton 1-0 as they had been the last side to win at East End. For the first time in seven seasons the match heralded the return of the TV cameras, though they later covered the Morton game too. The Premier League was almost all sewn up and the TV people probably thought that our style of play and atmosphere warrented a visit. Morrison's goal was crucial that day. We were now a staggering seven points clear of second-placed Morton and, when Norrie McCathie again presented us with a last minute goal at Clyde, thoughts of the Championship began to take root.

A freak snowstorm had put off the Morton verses Kilmarnock game, with the ironic result that I ended up as the expert analyst on BBC *Sportsound* when it came to be played midweek, and it was quite an experience trying to be objective when my heart told me I wanted Killie to win! In the event Morton did win, and deservedly so.

I was so pleased that the sudden media exposure seemed to have left the players unaffected, indeed it may have motivated them, but the 1-2 defeat by Morton was very disappointing. A win would have virtually clinched it but just when we were pressing for a winner Robertson toppled over Bobby Forrest's leg and we never recovered from their penalty. I felt it was now a good time to strengthen and we paid out £15,000 for Willie Irvine and £33,000 for Stuart Beedie from Hibs. Willie had always done well for Stirling against us, while we knew Stuart was a first-class player and would do a great job for us if his injury did not affect him. I felt new players might take some of the pressure off and knew I had to start building my squad for what seemed increasingly like a promotion place.

The East Fife game was a derby that was going to be as hard as ever despite Dave Clarke going to Falkirk along with Gordon Marshall. Willie Irvine scored with a vital penalty to gain a 1-1 draw and we learned that Morton had probably ended Dumbarton's hopes. Ominously, they were only two points behind. No team had ever won the Second and First Division titles back to back but we all knew that one point a game would be enough to gain promotion. Results had become more important than performance. Our next two games were quite a contrast, a 0-1 defeat to Kilmarnock and a superb 2-0 win at Partick. We lost an early goal in the former and were left chasing the game; in the latter Donnelly had a fine game and Stevie Morrison hit a remarkable 35-yard goal.

We could have wrapped up promotion at Brechin but in front of almost 5,000 we went down 0-2. At the final whistle the fans were

Don't you dare switch off, Gregor

*Players and officials set out on a well-deserved holiday after gaining promotion
to the Premier League*

outraged at the team's performance. Brechin should have won by at least four clear goals. It was probably Dunfermline's worst performance of the year and I felt pressure more at this time than anything, not for myself but for the players. We were so close yet so far away. But it was clear that the supporters in general were disgusted. Some even threw their scarves on to the pitch. Immediately I picked them up and put them round my neck, making a gesture that no matter what the result I would always be a Dunfermline fan and stick by the team.

On the Monday the press had caught hold of the story and the media coverage we received helped to ease the pressure. The stage was now set for probably the club's greatest victory since the late 1960s. Nothing less than a win against Queen of the South on 25 April 1987 would do. If we achieved this goal we would be the first Dunfermline Athletic team ever to play in the Premier League. No more was said or done in the build-up to the game – it wouldn't ease the pressure beforehand.

The players arrived before the match in good spirits. Despite the baking sun, I wore one of the scarves discarded by the fans the previous week. I was determined to make my point. The team seemed relaxed, but from three o'clock onwards it was a game of football that basically was not attractive to watch. The players were very nervous throughout and no matter what we shouted, no matter what instructions we gave, the players had to do this one on their own. I was sitting in the stand watching the game.

After we had scored through Willie Irvine, Queen of the South, rather than lying down and letting Dunfermline dominate, started to play attractive football and put us under tremendous pressure. Unfortunately for us we missed two good chances. The tension in the stand was unbearable, the fans grew impatient as they became more excited about the prospect of gaining promotion to the Premier League. With about 15 minutes to go Queen of the South were pushing forward, looking much more like a team that was going for promotion than a bottom of the League side. I got off my seat and I stood shouting at Bobby Forest to try and push forward more and hold the defence rather than sit tight and wait on Queen of the South equalising. In fact Gregor Abel later told me he had by this point switched off the walkie-talkie as my shouting was coming over loud and clear anyway! It made no difference. My heart seemed to be racing at one hundred times its

Well done, lads, you deserved the cheers!

normal pace. Minutes seemed like hours, but eventually the final whistle blew.

The tensions, the nerves, the anxiety, all drained from my body within seconds. I was so relieved for the whole town and for the directors and players. Tears of joy filled my eyes and no one, and I mean no one, was prouder than Jim Leishman at this particular time and moment. I went to the dressing-room where the players were singing and dancing. The scenes of joy were terrific to behold. After being chucked in the bath, opening the champagne, singing

The best support in the world

93

along with the players, getting photographs taken of everyone, I changed into a new suit, and again I was promptly thrown back into the bath! These are memories which will never be forgotten by me and everyone connected with the club.

Later the celebrations continued in the Paragon club at East End Park. The players and some fans ended up doing the conga through the streets of Dunfermline, the problem being that one or two of them in their excitement clambered over cars. Later I had to go down to the Police HQ to get two of my players out!

I had been sick on a few occasions as a three o'clock kick-off approached, now I was going to enjoy the occasion. After years of abject failure and disappointment we were back in the big time. Our reserves did us proud by winning the Reserve League East while three of our young lads, Strang, Williamson and Sinclair had made the under-18 Scotland team. But the season wasn't over yet. There was still a vital game at Airdrie to prepare for, then the final match at Montrose. If we won both we had done it!

Dunfermline's first ever Premier League squad, season 1987/88

Heading for glory: Ray Sharpe beats Paul Hamilton in this aerial duel at East End Park

As the roar went up from the black and white legions at Airdrie I held open the dressing-room door and said "That roar is for you. Go for it!" Airdrie were barely in the game in the first half, then we hit the post before McCall got a penalty which he converted. I thought we had done it but John Flood came on and scored two late goals. We were utterly depressed when we learned that Morton had gone to the top by beating Forfar.

But there was always the possibility that Morton themselves could come unstuck at Airdrie, and at Montrose we would be playing the Division's poorest team who were already relegated, We hadn't even lost a goal in taking every point off them.

There was a carnival atmosphere at the ground with more than 2,000 Pars fans travelling. There was no John Watson that day but Montrose had two trialists and a reserve 'keeper. They sneaked a goal just on half-time and I gave the lads one of the biggest rollick-ings, I've ever given in the interval. The supporters went daft when news broke that Morton were losing but we did not look likely to get one goal far less two and as we pressed forward Montrose almost exploited gaps at the back. No further goals were scored.

However, promotion was an achievement in itself and we ended up on 56 points, having won 11 games away to 12 at home. Our gates had almost reached 100,000 and no team outwith the Premier Division could come near to emulating that! Norrie McCathie had played in every game, Ian Westwater had 19 shut outs and John Watson was top goalscorer on 13. The year of "consolidation" had turned into a year of triumph!

Relegation 1987-88

There was a real buzz about East End when I came back from my holidays in Greece all set for our first season in the Premier Division. The air of optimism and anticipation was reminiscent of 20 years earlier. Structural alterations were moving apace and two new books on the remarkable achievement of moving from the backwater of Division Two to the glamour of the Premier Division had just been published. The mere handful of season tickets left available was further evidence of the upsurge in interest in the district.

Like Allan McGraw of Morton I knew only too well that the rewards for the club coming fourth bottom were going to be immense in a season when 25 per cent of the Premier's membership was going to end up relegated. I saw Motherwell, St Mirren, Falkirk and Morton as the others who would comprise our mini-league.

We were going to operate a pool of 16 full-time players, though by the end of the season I would have used 33 as the correct blend was sought. Having splashed out £50,000 for Stuart Beedie and Willie Irvine in the spring, another £75,000 had now been spent on bringing George Cowie from Hearts, Graeme Robertson from Queen of the South and Craig, his namesake, from a reluctant Raith Rovers. Cowie had played in the Cup semi-final and was an experienced utility player who had played under John Lyall at West Ham at one time, Graeme Robertson was Queen of the South captain and a pacy industrious right-back and, after three years of failing to get him, I had Craig, who would now have a Premier stage on which to show his undoubted talents. The media asked if I was falling into Hamilton's mistake of buying too many new players and I replied that Falkirk had bought a few and stayed up. I knew, of course, even then that many of the lads who had brought us up from Division Two so rapidly would be found out at this level but, in any case, we were not in a position to splash out millions to bring in quality players. What I had to spend would not have paid for a week's wages at Ibrox! I remember making the remark that we could now defeat Rangers and England on the same day – strangely it was actually to come true!

Although the bible of Scottish football *The Wee Red Book* insisted that we were still in Division One, 8 August was a fantastic day, a gala occasion. I had arrived at East End Park as usual on Saturday between 9 and 9.30 a.m. Everyone seemed to have a terrific sense of excitement. We were about to witness that afternoon the first ever Premier League match in Dunfermline's history. The players were to arrive at 1.45 p.m., the team had already been selected, the atmosphere was set for a gala occasion. My thoughts at the time were of sheer pride and I prayed that we could achieve the fourth bottom place so that we could avoid relegation. Two fifty-five p.m. that day was probably one of the most emotional times in my career at Dunfermline Football club and when the team left the dressing-room to go on to the park the instructions were, "Go to the middle of the park, line up and wave to the Dunfermline fans". The gesture was received with a tremendous ovation. 12,000 fans in shirt sleeves saluted the Pars! In the stand all the supporters stood up and clapped and cheered, while on the terracing the scarves were raised and the noise was deafening. The tears were full in my eyes – I was so proud of the lads that had achieved such a feat in just a year.

It was a great game and the scintillating 3-3 draw whetted the appetite for more. Two good draws at St Mirren and Falkirk and a 3-1 win at Firs Park in the Skol Cup set us up nicely for the classic encounter with Celtic at East End in front of a then capacity crowd of 18,070. We are kings of the treble chance, I declared that day in the programme, we are already in line for a place in Europe, all we can do now is throw it away! Another draw would, of course, have suited us, indeed I admitted it at the time, but it is history that in front of the cameras we pulled off a great 2-1 victory, with Ian Westwater having a blinder.

The evening before the Celtic game I had watched a television documentary on Martin Luther King and I was moved by the man and his faith. It rubbed off on me because when I had my team talk I spoke of my faith in Dunfermline Athletic. I said that I too had a dream – to see the club back where we belonged. I made it funny, of course, by saying to the players just before they went out on to the pitch, "Do you believe?" They roared back, "I believe, I believe." But my commitment to that dream was deeply felt!

In retrospect we were developing a false sense of security. Maybe the Premier Division was not so tough after all! "I don't want to take anything away from Dunfermline but Celtic were clearly the better team," remarked Billy McNeill. He was just about right, Celtic had taken nothing away from Dunfermline and Caesar had been buried! I felt the win was no fluke and only proved the character and commitment which everyone behind the scenes at East End knew existed.

Now there was to be another test. In the past the only way Dunfermline fans could have seen the likes of Souness, Butcher, Roberts and Woods at East End would have been if we were chosen to play World Cup warm-ups against Scotland and England. Now these international class players were to appear courtesy of the Skol Cup. The Pars programme named Roy Aitken at number four for

Courtesy of Dunfermline Athletic Football Club

Dunfermline 2 Celtic 1, it's magic: 22 August 1987

Rangers that night but that was one player they didn't have! With five league points out of eight and the Pars grabbing all the headlines, maybe pride came before a fall. In the event we were well beaten 1-4.

Our first home game had already attracted more spectators than the entire gate in my first season as manager. However, the truly brilliant performance of Ian McCall against the Old Firm had not gone unnoticed and, as I describe elsewhere, Rangers upped their bid no less than three times before he signed on the dotted line for £200,000. It easily beat the £60,000 paid for Alex Ferguson when he had taken the same journey two decades before. Ian had been called "Diego" by the fans both for the physical and playing similarities he shared with Maradona. He had a skilful left foot and his jinking runs, powerful shots, accuracy and ability to open up a defence were the reasons I was delighted to see him return in 1990. His goal at Ibrox against Hibs was to be a sensation. But 24 hours later, when my injury hit team went down 0-5 at Dens Park, a vocal minority of the fans jeered the move, attributing the awful defeat to the loss of one player. "I have sold an ace to buy four kings," was my immediate retort and I was able at last to snap up Billy Kirkwood and John Holt from Dundee United and Gary Riddell from Aberdeen while getting that great pro from Hibs, Bobby Smith; seeing him play a mere 15 minutes for Hibs reserves as sub convinced me that this extremely experienced player could do a job for the club, and so it was to prove.

The 5-0 thrashing by Dundee, a disappointing 0-1 defeat at the hands of experienced Motherwell and being taken apart 0-4 by Rangers did not leave much doubt that positions just had to be strengthened. A 4-1 win over Morton did relieve the gloom but there were to be six more defeats by late October. Along with Motherwell, Morton and Falkirk we were on the deck of a sinking ship looking enviously at the one lifebelt.

By this time we had signed Mark Smith from Celtic, a player we had been tracking since his Queen's Park days when he played with Ian McCall. His pace was breathtaking but he did not have the accuracy at crossing which had been "Ziggy" Bowie's trademark. We had Norwegian internationalist Vetle Anderson on trial, which pleased the young female fans no end. I called our Viking "Hagar the Horrible" which was no worse than him calling me "The Beach Whale"!

We were still not encountering a great deal of luck. A 1-0 defeat by Hearts had seen Craig Robertson miss a gilt-edged opportunity in the last ten seconds while we were doing fine at Pittodrie till Trevor Smith got himself sent off and we went on to lose 3-0. I was so annoyed I dashed into the dressing-room and felt like hitting him. We had been frustrating Aberdeen but thanks to Trevor we had missed the chance to get a result. I picked up a half-full bottle of lemonade but the top came off and the sticky liquid ran down the inside of my new jacket. I was not pleased! A few days later, before the midweek draw with Dundee United, I was in the dressing-room pounding my breast pocket with a clenched fist. "What am I doing?" I asked. "You are showing pride in the club badge," ventured John Holt. "No," I said. "It's your pride in the club which beats within your heart," suggested Bobby Smith. "No," I said again. I took out a photo from my pocket of Trevor, put it on the floor and jumped on it. "That's what it is," I smiled.

With the return of the influential Beedie and Watson there were consecutive wins over Morton and St Mirren and we remained in the position – just – which would ensure safety. The players who had brought us up from Divison Two were now disappearing fast; Bobby Forrest to Abroath, Rowan Hamilton to Brechin, Gary Thompson to St Johnstone, Grant Reid to East Fife and David Young to Airdrie, while John Donnelly, Willie Irvine and Eric Ferguson were now transfer-listed. That Christmas when the club's calendar came out we would be surprised to find Eric's face among the 11 other Dunfermline "greats"! We only sold 1,000 of the 5,000 copies ordered. It was Karen Grega's last "revenge"!

Ross Jack who had got off to such a great start with a Denis Law-style overhead kick in the 2-3 defeat at Fir Park, was now a regular in the team but it was to take him a while to establish himself as the potent goal scorer of the next two seasons. A lot of players had come and gone and it would take till later in the season for the team to blend.

We had Falkirk under virtual siege conditions with Gordon Marshall, as so often, performing heroics, including an incredible fingertip save from Mark Smith at the death. Celtic gained their revenge in a 4-0 defeat while the disappointment of yet another 2-3 defeat, this time at Tynecastle, suggested yet again that while the cavalier style was winning us lots of friends, it wasn't doing much for the points tally. One player having a magnificent season, however, was veteran Bobby Smith who had had an outstanding career at Leicester and Hibs and who had been a team-mate of mine in the Scottish under-18 amateur team. I was captain in three of those games and when I see the career he or Sandy Jardine or Kenny Dalglish had, I once more regretted the premature end to my career. Bobby was still winning a host of man of the match awards.

Ken McNaught joined the club, as another with top class experience under his belt with League and European Cup medals. I continued to believe in the Jock Stein maxim that the best form of defence is attack and I knew that Pars fans would not take kindly to defence in depth and three lines of markers strewn across the 18-yard box. However the Hearts game had provided food for thought. We had been written off before the game, a view reinforced when the deadly John Robertson scored, but a brilliant Craig Robertson equaliser followed by a Burns own goal set the scene for a 20-minute spell which resembled the seige of the Alamo.

McPherson and Clark scored in the last six minutes and on this occasion Goliath had smote David.

There followed the usual defeat by the Dons but in December we had a good spell. One of the most exciting goals of the season in one of the best games was the rocket shot by Craig Robertson after a brilliant run and cross by Beedie in a match in which Smith and Beedie had tormented Hibs on both flanks. There were 1-1 draws with Morton and Motherwell and a 32,000 crowd took in a magnificent 2-2 performance at Ibrox where the cavalier style was vindicated.

With Ian Westwater suffering whiplash in a car accident we were to have Tom Carson, Hans Segers and Dave McKellar in goal in subsequent months. By Christmas we were still in third equal bottom place and I was bemoaning the fact that whenever we strung a few results together so did the other teams in the relegation mire!

We faced the daunting prospect of meeting Hearts, Aberdeen and Celtic in the January (we were to lose all three) but for the moment the Ibrox result had bucked everyone up. Twice they had led but twice we had come back, with goals by Craig Robertson and Beedie. It should have served as a warning to them. Walter Smith, in fact, called it their worst performance of the year.

The two Cup-ties with Ayr were a pleasant break from the relegation pressure. For those fans who believe there is little passion, excitement or fervour outwith the top half of the Premier Division the two televised recordings of this Cup-tie would necessitate a rethink. More than 20,000 watched the two ties and they witnessed two crackers. To the sound of 2,500 Ayr fans singing their catchy *Super Ayr* song, which had some Pars fans feet tapping, Ayr had one attacking wave after another, with Templeton and Cowell showing why they were rated two of the most exciting players in that Division. Ross Jack scored against the run of play, then Walker scored when we were down to ten men. Ayr looked desperately tired and the game ended 1-1. Ayr may have convinced themselves that now they had the advantage but my lads were fully psyched up after two days at the Inverclyde Centre and goals by Jack and Smith saw us comfortably into the lucrative Cup-tie with Rangers.

With Motherwell galloping off into the sunset and five consecutive league defeats in which not one goal was scored (this grim record later went up to eight) relegation was looking probable.

A whole generation of Athletic fans had never experienced the atmosphere of a European tie at East End which was why we were delighted to welcome the French champions and European Cup quarter-finalists Bordeaux. Their team comprised of no less than nine internationalists and they played at East End in gloves and tracksuit bottoms. The papers called them "Bordeaux Chilled". They didn't play to their full potential but we still gained a creditable 1-1 draw when you consider they had players of the class of Dropsy, Tigana, the Vujuvic brothers and Ferreri in their team. It was a boost to win such a game on penalties.

I was now very concerned about the lack of goals and attempts were made to sign the likes of Portadown's O'Neill, St Mirren's McGarvey, Hamilton's Taylor and above all Ajax's Stapleton. I genuinely wanted Frank Stapleton but we could not even approximate the sort of wages he was used to.

As I mentioned, when the draw was made for the fourth round of the Scottish Cup the big news was that we had got Rangers. The whole of the Scottish media naturally wrote us off. We were only there apparently to make up the numbers. We were to be the lambs to the slaughter. I took my squad to prepare them at St Andrews. All the time we were there we had a quiet confidence and knew at the back of our minds that Rangers stars would probably underestimate us. I had every faith that the lads could do it and as I wondered what team talk to give I came upon the story of David and Goliath while browsing through the bible in my bath. That gained massive media coverage and Ian St John and Jimmy Greaves looked on in mock amazement as my home-made poetry readings were delivered to the players. "Oh Lord you know the dangers when my players take on the Rangers, Pars 2 Gers 1, what a thought, to beat that Souness man!"

The score was wrong but the sentiment was not too far out. 19,360 packed into East End that day with media presence to match. The players did not require any motivation. My team was McKellar, G. Robertson, McCathie, Holt, Anderson, C. Robertson, Beedie, R. Smith, M. Smith, Watson, Jack, subs Ferguson and Kirkwood. The game was fast and furious from the very start and my underdogs rose superbly to the occasion. The game was set alight in the opening minutes when Mark Smith got on the end of a Craig Robertson pass and avoided the offside trap. He left Jan Bartram for dead and lofted over an incredible cross which left international goalie Chris Woods stranded as the ball flew over his head into the net – memories of Kevin Gallacher at Tannadice!

I wonder how often Pars fans have played that tape on video! Here was the player who for so long had had trouble finishing off a dazzling run with an accurate cross and his goal would now be one of the greatest the club had ever seen. He tried to convince me later that he had meant it too!

Our defence was now under ferocious pressure but Anderson, McCathie and Holt performed heroics. Just on half time Rangers were reduced to ten men when John Brown clashed with Mark. Any fear that Rangers might come back and ruin our afternoon evaporated four minutes into the second half. It was a coaching move from our training ground which clinched it too. A beautifully accurate corner from Stuart Beedie was touched on by Mark Smith at the near post and John Watson ran in to head spectacularly past Woods as the Rangers defence stood like statues.

We were now put under enormous pressure and I was glad I was not wearing a watch as there were many close things, yet Rangers too were vulnerable to a quick break and Beedie and Mark Smith gave relief by exploiting that whenever they could. Finally the whistle went and I had another photo of an ecstatic leap from my dugout for my collection. I had felt that treating the players to a wee bit of luxury at the sort of venue Sean Connery or Jack Nicklaus take for granted would be a psychological boost and so it had proved. No one later quibbled with £1,300 expenses. When you plot a match in the Royal Suite you tend to create a craving for more of the same. The reshuffled defence had worked wonders and we had guessed correctly the Gers formation once it was confirmed McCoist was missing. Mark meanwhile picked up the Mr Superfit award and almost collapsed later!

The subsequent quarter-final against Hearts was to be a complete anti-climax and we were totally outplayed in the 3-0 defeat. We had wanted a home draw but it was not to be. I told the media, and I meant it, that I would gladly have swapped that great Cup result – our best since 1968 – for a place in the Premier League. Every game would now be a cup final. We hadn't scored in eight league games and were a staggering seven points adrift of safety.

After such disappointment in front of a 22,000 crowd we could hardly have anticipated a 6-1 victory over Dundee but that is just what happened, with Craig notching up another two on the way to

John Watson scores Pars' second goal against Rangers in the SFA Cup, 20 February 1988

The statement was to prove correct. What a great day, the last day of the season at Parkhead for Celtic after winning the Premier League Championship, 7 May 1988

his remarkable record of being the highest scoring midfielder in Scotland. Hopes were raised by a great 3-0 display at Cappielow but another 2-3 defeat at Motherwell in a game where we led at one point by two goals ended it. We were still to have two commendable draws, 1-1 with Aberdeen and 2-2 at Dundee Utd, and we defeated St Mirren but the dream for the moment was at an end.

A large number of fans went through to Parkhead and joined in the Celtic birthday party. ''We'll be back'' was displayed defiantly on a few banners. The Premier Division was the only place to be. We had come a long way very fast but had learned from the experience and would be prepared next time.

Chapter 6

THE CHAMPIONS AT LAST!

Walking down the Halbeath Road to see the Leishman's Aces
To see the Athletic fans with smiles upon their faces
First Division champions made them very proud
Championees! championees! they would sing out loud
Every Saturday they would watch Dunfermline play
Championees! championees! Away! Away! Away!

THE date 13 May 1989 was one of the happiest times of my life and will always remain one of the most important days in the history of Dunfermline Athletic Football Club. It was the day the club won its first Division One Championship trophy and was the culmination of all the hard work which had gone on all season.

The pressure of the last week, after the disappointing 1-1 draw with Clyde, was truly horrendous and I rarely slept a wink as the big day approached. If we failed in that one match I was only too aware there would have to be major changes. A vast amount of money had been gambled on success in one season and to finance another full-time season in the lower division there would have to be sackings and players allowed to go. The revenue lost from games like the Old Firm, Aberdeen and the Edinburgh clubs simply could not be made up by commercial ventures. Everything would have to be rethought.

I was up that morning at five o'clock and I tried everything I could to get my mind off it. I went for a walk, then came in and did some vacuum cleaning! I drove to East End at nine to get a feel for the atmosphere. I felt I handled the media well. I told them that whatever the result, Jim Leishman would always be proud to walk up the High Street with these players. The players had given their all during the season. They had come back from all the injuries and suspension and had survived the incredible pressure. We just had to succeed.

At that time in the morning, I had a blether with the groundstaff and the tea ladies, and found they were caught up in the emotion too. They were all worried sick about what would happen. By noon I was being physically sick. I had no relief till about one-thirty when the players began to arrive and they appeared to be at ease. They were handling things well and knew only too clearly what was at stake. The club had never won the Championship before.

I put the team sheet out at one-thirty. Gary Riddell was very disappointed but no one would celebrate more afterwards. My team that day was Westwater, G. Robertson, R. Smith, McCathie, Tierney, Sharp, Beedie, P. Smith, Jack, Watson, Irons, substitutes M. Smith and Gallacher. I pointed out in the programme that it was one of the most important days in the club's history and I implored the fans to get right behind us to help take some of the pressure off. I knew that Meadowbank had escaped the drop and there would be nothing for them to lose. That was just how it worked out.

From the moment the game began the Pars players clearly had the jitters again, just like the previous Saturday. No matter what instructions were roared from the dugout, the atmosphere and the occasion were getting to them. The crowd of 12,976 were giving all they had but the players' nerves had got to them. We kept hearing that Falkirk were doing well at Station Park against Forfar and I kept shouting that I didn't want the players to know.

Then, in the 62nd minute, the unthinkable happened. Former Pars favourite Bobby Forrest crossed and Gordon Scott put it away. The dream of our first Division One Championship in our 104-year history seemed to be evaporating. Bobby Forrest had his head in his hands while Scott did not accept congratulations, but that was no consolation. We had hit woodwork twice and John Watson had unaccountably been called back for a free kick when clean through on the goalkeeper. A number of thoughts went through my mind – Denis Law scoring the City goal that finally relegated Manchester United, Hearts at Dens Park, the Sunday papers headlines saying "Falkirk Champions" or "Falkirk steal it at the death" or "Pars blow it"!

*Wasn't all the hard work worth it? First Division Champions at last,
13 May 1989*

Then luck, which in a season of long-term injury and suspension had seemed conspicuous by its absence, suddenly smiled on the players in black and white. Blond full-back Graeme Robertson, a model of consistency, hit a long ball down the right. Boyd failed to cut it out and John Watson, with quite incredible coolness (and I am glad it was he and no one else), drew McQueen and slotted home the golden goal. The relief cannot be put into words. Momentarily I feared it might be offside. One thing's for sure, we weren't going to take issue with the linesman when his flag stayed down! John Watson had no doubt and the celebrations began. It had seemed to take ages from John controlling the ball to hitting the back of the net! We never looked like losing after that and news began to filter through that high-scoring Falkirk had got into difficulties in the last game at Forfar.

I didn't even consider committing a substitute but the last 22 minutes seemed to last for hours. When Mr Evans of Bishopbriggs flamboyantly signalled the end, scenes unequalled since the 1968 Cup final ensued. No one will ever take away the sight of all the happy faces around me and the feeling of relief. We were now in the record books. I was desperate that the players and people like Pip Yeates and Joe Nelson should get the accolade so, after the luxury of a quick glance up at Mary and my family in the stand, I nipped into the dressing-room. As I came out I felt like Zeus, up in the clouds. I could have climbed Mount Everest without climbing gear or swum the channel without any flippers! As I came out the scenes of sheer, unadulterated joy were amazing. I was given a scarf, then a huge plastic champagne bottle – with nothing in it! I was as high as a kite, and dashing around the track pretending to be an aeroplane was at least apt. I was grabbed by the media. "Pressure? What pressure?" I enquired of *Scotsport*'s Jim White, tongue in cheek. I had not wanted to get the title through Falkirk's failure, I wanted to achieve it as of right, and we had.

Then came the greatest moment. Bobby Smith, the captain, who had had such an outstanding season for us, was presented with the trophy, an unforgettable moment. A lot of people ended up in the bath naturally, as the fans drifted home for their own celebrations. Jim White, Mel Rennie and myself were unceremoniously tossed in before the multitude of empty champagne bottles took up too much space! Eventually we went downstairs to talk to all the guests and sponsors, then there were more media interviews for the Sunday headlines. Seeing the Paragon Club filled to capacity was a terrific sensation.

A lot of players had already left by the time I tried to get away, but as I left I noticed near the entrance a stunning young lady who gave me a beaming smile. "Could I have your autograph on such a great day?" she asked. Always willing to oblige a fan, I looked for the book as I took out my pen. "Where am I to sign?" I asked curiously. "Here," she replied lifting up her top and showing a pair of large boobs! I did wonder at that moment if Mary was somewhere behind me!

I caught up with the players at Cagney's, the pub owned by Norrie McCathie and John Watson. It was jam-packed, as busy as the London rush hour. Then it was off to join up with more supporters at the East Port Bar, where we sang all the usual football songs all over again. Then we joined the Pitbauchlie Travel Club and ended up at Noddy's Neuk. I was beginning to feel like the pied piper! I left there at half past midnight and still didn't want the day to end. I was hoarse from singing and sat on the wall with a bottle of champagne. I remember a police Panda car drew up. "Are you

First Division Champions, the squad that was to keep us in the Premier League

okay?'' an officer enquired. But I wasn't drunk, just totally and utterly elated.

I must tell you a story about the start of that season. On 19 July, when we had barely started training, we were trounced 6-0 by Girondins de Bordeaux in a small stadium at Trelissac in France. What an adventure that turned out to be! Even now I would call it "Trains and Boats and Planes". Let me explain why.

It was, to begin with, a much anticipated trip. It had been arranged by travel agent Bonar Mercer, a pal and former Pars player in the 1970s. What he was not to know was that there would be a strike that week by French air traffic control. We had to take a flight to London, coach from Heathrow to Victoria, train to Dover and then ferry to Calais. On the ferry it was absolutely teeming down outside and we realised that Joe Nelson was missing. There was some concern so I began to look around the deck. Suddenly I found him sitting alone on a deckchair in a waterproof, looking greener than Peter Grant! He had his false teeth out and I couldn't even talk for creasing myself. He looked so sorry for himself.

Next the train from Calais to Paris arrived an hour late as we missed our connection and Jimmy McConville had to book a hotel in the city at the last gasp. We then had to push all our bags and suitcases on top of porters' trolleys along the street to the hotel. And the hotel, arranged at short notice, was like something out of a Boris Karloff movie. You went up and down the different floors two or three at a time in what seemed to be more of a cage than a lift. I had to walk around on crutches as I'd just had a bad leg operation, but that came in handy for attacking a rat the following day!

We knew that day that we had to be all set to go at 9.45 for the coach taking us to the station. As a group of us ambled back to the hotel at my speed on crutches, we saw Jimmy waving at us like mad to speed up. "What's their panic?" I said. "The coach can't go without us!" "Yes it can," answered Jimmy with ill-concealed exasperation in his voice. "It's public transport!" I hobbled as fast as possible but, with Joe and Ian, duly missed the coach. Thankfully, the courier said she'd give us a lift and we managed to catch up with the coach at traffic lights. But then once more relief turned to alarm when we saw Steve Morrison signal that two players were missing – at least I think that explained the two fingers! Neither Holt nor Jack would have their cash or passports. Fortunately John had been in Paris a few days earlier as a reward for being club Player of the Year so knew his way around. They eventually caught us up. Jimmy was on about the fact that we had not returned the hotel key but with things becoming increasingly fraught I told him to "shove it"!

Next on this epic journey we faced the six-hour train journey to Bordeaux. Thankfully, the directors cheered us up. They had a few drinks and that culminated in Mr Braisby doing a superb take-off of a French ticket collector asking for fares. This gave us a laugh and was taken in good part by the French passengers. Perhaps predictably, though, when we arrived in the sweltering heat there was no coach to meet us as we were so late. That was eventually sorted out and we ended up with excellent accommodation and superb training facilities.

In the match itself we somehow managed to do well for 50 minutes against a top class team including Dropsy, Tigana and Clive Allen but we dropped like flies after that – hence the scoreline.

That August I knew we were in for a very hard season in Division One and this is what I said in the opening programme:

Another season is underway and no doubt all of you are feeling, as I am, the special buzz of anticipation that footballers love in August. This season more than most there is a feeling of expectancy to make

112

sure of promotion come May. Nothing would please me more than to make a quick return to the Premier League and I'm sure that the fans, having experienced it last season, agree that it is the place for Dunfermline to be. Achieving that aim, though, is going to be very difficult in a very competitive division with five or six very good sides playing against us.

There was a lot of talk last year about the fact that with three clubs going down the Premier League was the toughest and most demanding in years. I believe that this year is going to be even tougher. Being a big club and a full-time outfit other teams will want to beat us even more than usual and the assumption by some that we will just go straight back up puts even more pressure on. Make no mistake though, the players, myself and all the backroom staff will be doing our level best to give the fans the standard of football, and results, that they expect and deserve.

A high level of commitment and dedication to the club is also very important to me and I expect the same commitment from the players on the park that the fans show by turning out every week rain or shine to support Dunfermline. If the team plays as well as it can then I am confident that we can more than match all the other sides in the First Division and win promotion. If there is any let up, however, there are plenty of good, ambitious sides who would be happy to step in and take the promotion spot which everyone associated with Dunfermline wants very much.

Relegation had been very disappointing, for all it was evident for some months that it was coming. Now I knew that every team would be gunning for us. We were full-time and by far the biggest team in the Division with the largest gates and backed by the enviable Eagle Glen training facilities. Every game was going to be a cup final. We had not had the resources to cope with the Premier Division but we had finished the season with something of a run. Hence the lack of lots of new faces in August 1988. I believed I had the nucleus of the team that would do it. All the bookies quoted us favourites from the off at 5-2. Then they reckoned Falkirk, Clydebank, Morton and Airdrie in that order. My own view was that the main threat would come from Falkirk, with Airdrie and Partick not too far behind. I would not be far out.

From the opening game at Firhill, where we pulled off a commendable 1-2 win, we were hammered by injuries and suspensions. We had five regulars out of the game including McCathie with a broken ankle. I also knew there would be a problem with the lack of atmosphere at certain away grounds and I cannot thank our magnificent travelling support enough for the noise they created at these venues. Most players rose to overcome the lack of atmosphere but when John Holt left he cited that as a main reason.

Three Skol Cup games against Motherwell and Hearts ended in an excellent 2-1 win, followed by a 4-1 hammering, but whetted the appetite for the big time again. We had prepared well for the Hearts game but ended up well beaten. We had looked the best team in the first half but lost a stupid goal. John Watson hit a shot over the bar with only the 'keeper to beat and with that our fate was sealed.

In between we defeated Raith 2-1 in the local derby. These games are always a special occasion and I recall one game against Raith in the days of Bobby Wilson as manager when on the Friday evening I got a phone call at home purporting to come from a Glasgow football reporter. He asked all about our hopes for the following day's game, our team plans and tactics, but I began to get suspicious of the detailed questions and what seemed to be the occasional giggle. It was, of course, Bobby doing it for devilment! Now Frank Connor, my old mate, was in charge and later in the season, during the crucial run in, Raith would become only the second team to defeat us at home all season.

Not only were our gates doing well but the BBC decision to televise games from Division One and Two was to be a much-needed boost to our League. A 2-1 defeat at Brockville reinforced my view that they were the main threat. Falkirk aways made things difficult – they knew our team and tactics seemingly inside out, and we hadn't even scored against them in 1987-88, which probably gave them a psychological advantage. I was also concerned that in the Division where you met your opponents three times, we were to meet them twice away. Indeed we lost both! At the end of a long season when we were faltering and Falkirk were having huge wins Jim Duffy remarked, "If only we could play Dunfermline at home again!"

I was saddened by the news that George Cowie had to give up the game. We had only signed him from Hearts in the May of 1987. He came up to my house with his wife and "Casper", as he was affectionately known, told me the bad report from the doctors. Hearts later agreed to a Testimonial game. A committee was formed under Audrey Kelly and the club gave him excellent support.

114

Bobby Smith receiving the First Division Championship Award,
13 May 1989

By September I was delighted to sign Paul Smith. I had been impressed with him back in his Raith days and it had not gone unoticed that he played spendidly in attack or midfield for Motherwell. He had a great attitude, was a grafter and could get a vital goal. At first I used him up front with Watson and then, when John could move from centre-back again, in midfield. He had had a great partnership with Keith Wright and scored 58 goals in the process before Tommy McLean snapped him up. With four Smiths now in my first team I joked with the media that all I had to do was roar from the dugout "get the finger out Smith" for things to happen!

Trevor Smith was having a great spell at the time, rounded off with a spectacular home goal against Partick in a 3-2 win. A 1-0 win over Airdrie in October was crucial and the following week we scored our 4,000th league goal at Ayr. A 1-3 home hammering by Meadowbank and 1-0 away defeat by Morton, who had made a great start, put us under real pressure. Going into November we had slipped to sixth place. Not only that but Meadowbank had ruined my fifth anniversary at the club. A succession of draws did not encourage hopes of promotion and I decided to tell the fans by way of the programme not to panic. I felt that our luck had to turn while the full-time training would eventually tell. With Norrie McCathie on the sidelines for so long we had to move John Watson into defence where he performed admirably but we missed his fire power up front.

Then came the turning point. We travelled to Perth to meet St Johnstone. In the papers the only Division One manager tipping us for promotion was Terry Christie. Morton were slipping and Falkirk, Clydebank, Airdrie and our opponents were now the bookies' favourites! St Johnstone are always a hard team to play. They had a number of seasoned professionals, some of whom at one time were Pars players and that added bite. They always cause us problems but we came away with a vital 0-1 result and although Alex Totten publicly slated our tactics we never looked back. We won eight of the next nine games and only slipped up 2-1 at Forfar.

A lot was now happening on the transfer front. We had brought Hugh Burns from Hearts at first on loan but later we signed him. He was a great character who was to do an important job for us, although I felt that emotionally he had never left the 'Gers. It was to prove a barrier for him. We lost Craig Robertson to Aberdeen and, as I explained elsewhere, we could hardly have stood in his way. We needed the cash to ensure promotion while the boy had the opportunity to go to a major club. There was despondency among the fans and indeed in the dressing-room at first but it freed the funds at last to move for Grant Tierney whom I had tracked for a considerable time. He was to develop, in my view, into the best centre-back in Division One! Terry Christie did not want to lose a key player, needless to say, and would not budge on the fee he had in mind – so we just had to meet it. Ironically his first game would be away to Meadowbank. On the Friday evening he had just listened intently to Terry meticulously making detailed plans to defeat us again and on the Saturday morning I was asking him to tell us all he knew! Grant said later that during the game he had sometimes got confused about whom to pass the ball to!

The 5-1 win at home to Ayr was thrilling for the fans but also testimony to the entertaining way Ally McLeod prepares for any game. There's no way he'll turn up with a boring defensive back five. Ayr had cracking players in Templeton, Sludden and Evans

Leave some for us, gaffer

and it was a relief to play so well at Christmas, thereby setting up a cracker with Falkirk. I was a relieved man that festive period.

At Hogmanay we were one point adrift of the Bairns with 27 points from 20 games. Three points separated the top five in what had always been predicted as a close contest. I felt it was going to be the match of the day – nothing in the Premier League could touch it – and in the event 12,889, one of the biggest ever Division One gates, agreed. The papers called it a league decider which was nonsense but there was no denying that the 3-0 victory was one of the most important and enjoyable of the whole season. In recent years a fierce rivalry has developed between the two clubs, with the result that in all honesty there is now an atmosphere at these games that even a Fife derby cannot match. The two clubs' fanzines slag each other regularly and on this occasion they sent me some balloons which I took in good heart. I avoided the temptation of bursting them in the dugout after the game! Gordon Marshall, who is usually an excellent goalie and so often a thorn in our flesh, had a rare poor game and we ended the year top of the league. Now we had to stay there!

Meanwhile Physio Pip Yeates committed himself to East End and gave up Sigourney Weaver's thighs for the endless collection of our crocks lined up at his treatment room. I did wonder about his state of mind!

Well, I hadn't had to really motivate the players for the Falkirk game as they knew full well what was at stake. The luck stayed with us when we pulled off a flattering 3-1 win at Stark's Park in the New Year derby. Then one of the best results of the season was a 2-0 win at Airdrie which substantially reduced the Diamonds' chances. I brought in Motherwell's Ray Farningham as a replacement at last for Craig Robertson and he had an excellent debut. The former Forfar player had been a model of consistency for the Fir Park team and I felt his main strength would be accurate crosses. On one later occasion I slammed him for the poor quality of his crosses. "Who does he think I am?" he later asked the other players. "Jinky?" The name stood.

The Cup game with Aberdeen was a marvellous break from the tension of the League and I tried every trick I knew to psyche out Alex Smith and his team of quality players. The main plan was to appear to be doing little other than relaxing whenever the media filmed us at Dunblane Hydro. It almost worked. We performed magnificently in the 0-0 draw at East End watched by a 17,000 crowd and the cameras and Pars fans will never forget the two incredible saves from Ross Jack by Theo Snelders. Before the game there was little necessity to motivate the players but in all the nervous tension I recall saying to the lads in the dressing-room, "Remember whatever you do today, you've done so well to get to this stage!" "What do you mean, it's only the first round?" they laughed! We eventually went down 1-3 in the replay at Pittodrie where an early goal sank us. I was honoured to receive my second manager of the month award and felt it reflected on the whole club.

Consecutive wins against Clyde 3-1, St Johnstone 1-0, Clydebank 1-0 followed these big matches and all seemed to be going smoothly. We were guarding against writing off the lesser opposition and still three teams were separated by four points. Bobby Smith made his 500th appearance in top class football.

We had opened up a useful three-point gap then we were thrashed 4-0 at Falkirk and lost 0-1 at home to Raith. We were outplayed in the former. We had considered playing a tight defensive game but on the evening decided to "go for it". A lot of players chose the same day to have their poorest game.

Mr Rennie with the ball that clinched promotion to the Premier League

Eddie Gallacher, who had been a top scorer in his days at Partick, came in a player swap with Stevie Morrison who moved to Hamilton. He had made over 200 appearances for us since 1981 but his first team games had become limited by then.

Meanwhile, alarm bells were sounding again. Jim Duffy's team had won three games in the last 12 and had regarded the game with us as their last chance. Now we had thrown them a lifeline. The defeat against Raith had come at a bad time. A crucial 2-0 win at Dumfries followed but three successive draws against Kilmarnock, Partick and nine-man Airdrie gave us all sleepless nights. The 1-0 win over Morton and 2-1 win at Ayr brought us to the run in one point clear of Falkirk, five clear of Airdrie, and those two were to meet at Broomfield.

We threw everything we had at Forfar's Stewart Kennedy but the light blue defence held. The players were spurred to new heights as the Pars fans made it clear that the Bairns were having an unhappy afternoon. Not for the first time they had become our extra man! I brought Beedie on for Farningham and Stuart, making his much awaited come back, had a blinder. A screamer of a shot by Davie Irons seemed to have almost settled the Championship and the fans

119

had an enjoyable drive home. "Do you know," said the Forfar secretary later, "that 3,301 crowd was not only the biggest gate here in more than 20 years but we've taken more today at the bridie stall than we took in gate receipts in the previous home game?" At least they hadn't run out of them!

We could have won the League against Clyde but didn't and that set up the jittery though memorable last game against Meadowbank. We were back in the Premier League and with our stadium, full-time set up, history, location, training HQ, crowds and ambition, where else should a big club like Dunfermline be? Some critics argue that simply because we had a large crowd and loyal support, we did not have a divine right to be in the top division but I would suggest the media, other club's treasurers and the shopkeepers in the towns the Athletic visit might just take issue with them.

Chapter 7

SURVIVAL SPECIAL

Our aim's this season to stay in the top ten
We're not wanting to fail and get relegated again
To survive this year we'll put up a great fight
No matter what happens, we'll get it right
If we stick together we'll achieve our glory
And go down in history as another success story
Promotion last year was difficult to gain
During the season often going insane
First Division champs now was our honour
Playing against McStay and the likes of Bonner
The team, the fans were back at the top
Together we'll stand rather than flop
Our history and traditions will see us through
For the people of Dunfermline this time for you

RAISING the First Division flag before our opening Premier match
with Dundee was a very proud moment for the club. However,
while I had no doubts about our ability to stay up, I was under no
illusions about the difficulties ahead. Our team spirit was excellent
but we were going to have to transfer this positive attitude on to
the park.

I knew the players' mental attitude was right. When they had
returned for their first agonising training session in late July – not
as early as some other clubs, so they did not peak too soon – they
were angry young men. With little other football news to report,
the papers were indulging, as they tend to, about the season ahead,
and a few printed the league positions for "May 1990". There were
minor variations in the order of the bottom four but one constant

was that Dunfermline always came bottom. The pride of my players was hurt. It was true that many clubs who had come up from Division One had simply returned whence they had come – Hamilton, Kilmarnock, Dumbarton, St Johnstone, Dundee and indeed even Hearts had already done so – but some journalists had pointed out that we were unlikely to prove "the insurance policy" which Hamilton had become. Teams like Hearts and Hibernian had become far too big for the lower division and that was a situation Dunfermline wanted to emulate. We now had that intangible quality called experience – something which clubs like Motherwell and St Mirren had in abundance and which had clearly stood them in good stead. We had a much stronger squad than in 1987 and the cavalier style of that period which won us lots of friends but not a lot of points would have to be abandoned. There was also considerable experience throughout our team and this was to rub off on the younger players. Jimmy Nicholl's pedigree included Manchester United and Rangers while Doug Rougvie had seen it all with Aberdeen and had played in a European Cup Winners' Cup final.

One key player, I felt, was going to be Stuart Rafferty, who was part of the Beedie deal. I had known that Stuart was unsettled and was not getting a regular game. I had first enquired about him when Dave Smith was Dundee manager. He had had five seasons at Motherwell, then five at Dundee where he had played in a Scottish Cup semi-final, so he knew the ropes. He was a good pro who would work hard on and off the park – most importantly, he could play football. As the season progressed I felt he was our most under-rated player by people outside the club and no one was to prove a more consistent player.

In contrast to all this experience was a £200,000 striker from Bordeaux, George O'Boyle, who had joined them from Linfield. He had been voted Young Footballer of the Year in Northern Ireland by both the Press and fellow professionals, was already being considered for the Irish squad by Billy Bingham and he was to prove a brilliant foil to Ross Jack, scoring four times himself in the process.

On the eve of the new season I had a serious talk to the players. I reminded them of what we had achieved the previous season, the pressures we had been under, what the flag had meant to the area, and I asked them, "Are we really going to throw it all away?" I tried to concentrate their minds on the fact that relegation would

Courtesy of Dunfermline Athletic Football Club

Mr Rennie, and the Provost of Dunfermline unfurling the First Division Championship flag, 12 August 1989

have a devastating effect on their standards of living. I stressed from the outset that we were in a mini-league of Hibernian, St Mirren, Motherwell and Dundee and we would have to fight to take points off these four. Any points off the top three would be an added bonus. It had been our abject failure against bottom clubs in 1987-88 which had led to our downfall.

Despite losing the first goal and having Jimmy Nicholl sent off we defeated Dundee in that opening game 2-1. It gave us a psychological advantage over them from the start and one which we never really lost all season. Ten days later we would put them out of the Skol Cup 1-0. In between, there had been the potentially difficult game with First Division Raith Rovers. It doesn't matter where our two teams are when we meet, these games are real derbies with all the passion that is generated. Frank Connor would have his team all fired up and well motivated to do well. I stressed to my players that we had to compete and that if we matched their standard of competitiveness then our superior standard of fitness would gradually take over. Raith were keen to put one over us, especially with our being Premier League, but we also fancied revenge for the

1-0 defeat at East End the preceding March and in the event we won comfortably 3-0.

Our pace, fire power and sheer all-out effort were coming to the attention of the media. Team spirit was good and two other factors reinforced that. First, we lost 0-1 at Parkhead and 1-2 at Tannadice but the large legion of travelling supporters knew the lads had given their all and the thunderous ovation they received at the end made them even more determined to reward the fans. Second, a great night was just around the corner.

On 29 August we were due to meet Hibernian in the quarter-final of the Skol Cup at Easter Road. We had not beaten Hibs in the Cup since that great game at Tynecastle in the 1965 semi-final when the papers had predicted beforehand "an all green final". Yet our paths had crossed repeatedly. In 1976 Dunfermline had played gallantly in round three and lost 2-3. In 1979 we drew 1-1 in that same round but lost at Easter Road 0-2 on an evening when I'd swear the seagulls had overcoats on. In 1981 we drew 1-1 away only to lose 1-2 at East End. In 1986 and 1987 we had put up excellent performances and lost 0-2. It's not surprising the fans were desperate after our poor performance in the last quarter-final appearance when we had lost 0-3 at Tynecastle to Hearts. I felt we were more experienced now and I told the players all the pressure would be on Hibs. They were playing in front of their own fans, the media had tipped them to win and they also had their minds on Europe. I told the lads that if we could contain Houchen, Collins and Kane on the night then we had a real chance.

It was to prove a great night, and a vindication for the system of playing three centre-backs with two overlapping full-backs. Rougvie scored early on, McCathie was outstanding and Tierney was to have one of his greatest games. There was pressure on when Collins equalised but the team held steady. They just had to hold on to the final whistle and they would make it. I simply told the lads just one more big effort, keep working, don't give the ball away, go into extra time on a positive note. They've thrown all they can at us and we are still level. Well, it is history that Paul Smith got us the vital goal. He had a great season and fans were never aware of just how vital a player he is. His goals and workrate, and tremendous enthusiasm make up for any lack of ability. However, the icing on the cake and, no doubt the fans' abiding memory of a great night, was that last-minute goal by Ross Jack, a rocket shot that beat international goalkeeper Andy Goram all ends up. Gallacher took the ball for a run down the left, he passed inside and with us all roaring to take it in on the goalie, Ross just let fly – and then celebrations began.

The Hampden semi-final, our first since 1969, was an awful anti-climax as we were thumped 0-5 by Rangers. The mass media coverage was great for the town and the players. There was such a feeling of pride. At the final whistle I felt it had passed us by all too quickly. Maybe it was the fact it was not at East End or perhaps there was no danger that Rangers would underestimate us after we had defeated them 2-0 in that sensational Cup-tie. Now I had to lift the players again and I reminded them that the bread and butter league games were still more important.

Our ambition had already been underlined with the signing of that exciting Magyar Istvan Kozma. What a contrast with my battle to raise the £2,000 for Allan Forsyth – Istvan would cost us £600,000, an incredible sum for a provincial club. He had cost Bordeaux that sum from Ujpest Dozsa and already had 16 inter-national caps. Having got a work permit he made his debut in the 1-1 draw with Motherwell (only ten non-EC players can play in Scotland at one time). The Bordeaux coach said that with the right preparation and training he would become a top European star and he could play as a defender or midfielder. However the French club had too many *étrangers* (Olsen, Den Boer, Alofs and Katz) and the French FA only allow a club three foreigners so their loss was our gain. The board was delighted as they knew we had got a top class player on a down payment. I called him Stevie Wonder and soon he and his family were settled here. There was just the one problem. He had no English whatsoever. On the way over on the plane he spoke in French to director Blair Morgan, who translated that from English – and then into "Kelty"! When he scored a hat-trick in the epic 5-1 home defeat of St Mirren it was one of the best hat-tricks East End has ever witnessed and each goal was better than the one which preceded it.

Well, on that first day when Istvan and I reached Dunfermline and Blair left, we were both tired and famished from the long journey so I took him for a meal at St Margaret's restaurant. The menu meant nothing to him. What was I to do? I began pointing at it and making farmyard noises. He shook his head, pork was out. then I began going, "Moo, moo." That was of no interest either.

In the end, in desperation, I got up on my seat and imitated a hen. It startled the other diners but Istvan smiled gratefully. We had chicken!

As the year went on, Istvan's progress in English was remarkable. We took him regularly for language lessons at an Edinburgh College where his tutor, who naturally had no Hungarian, taught him English by using a puppet. It was so novel an approach that Jim White featured it later on *Scotsport*. We also had the welcome help of interpreter John Domokos who would report to East End on a match day and help in putting across our tactics and game plan. To Istvan's credit we went from sign language to remarkably fluent conversation and his wife Ildiko made similar progress. They grew to love the town as time went on.

The victory over St Mirren was part of a magnificent eight-game unbeaten run which effectively set us up for the remainder of the season. The first game against Rangers was the most important as I had to lift the players after the huge disappointment of the Cup game against the same club in midweek. There was only to be one change in my team. The newspapers had said that we had stood back and admired Rangers. We analysed the game and I made the point that we could not allow that to happen again. We got a creditable 1-1 draw against a team packed with internationalists. Everyone had kept their concentration and contributed to the best of their ability.

That game was followed with a remarkable brace by full-back Graham Robertson giving us a welcome point against Hibs, scene of an earlier triumph, when Hibs were fresh from their best European result in more than 20 years. Then we pulled off a magnificent 2-1 result at Tynecastle. Hearts would only lose four times at home all season, and we were to pull off a remarkable double. It took me back to that game in 1974 when we had last won there and I had been told to mark Donald Ford. We soaked up enormous pressure, the players gained in confidence and they carried out my demand that they play to their strengths and "show what you can do". Games like that and the defeat of St Mirren were a hint, I felt, of better days to come. The players began to remark that to mention the word "relegation" in the same breath as Dunfermline was starting to look silly. All season I never used the word relegation once, not once!

The following 2-1 win at Dens Park was so important because

they were starting to go through a sticky patch and we had to adopt a professional attitude and not show any sympathy. Then we beat Celtic 2-0 at home, one of the highlights of any season, but I remember warning my players afterwards that the "Old Firm never forget". We had learned that lesson with a vengeance at the Skol Cup semi-final. In any case, we all realised that the Dundee win was far more important. By the time we drew 1-1 with Dundee United in early November, I was having to appeal to the fans to keep their feet on the ground. I was getting concerned that there was ludicrous talk that we were now aiming for a place in Europe, that we were safe from relegation or would do as well as Hearts in 1986. It was nonsense and the fans were putting unwanted additional pressure on the players. It was to last a bit longer, the 1-1 draw with Motherwell putting us on top of the division, a position we had not been in since 1965, if only for a few days. As the supporters celebrated on the terracings I was giving the players a roasting in the dressing-room. The performance had been dreadful. The following day, though, we did take time to analyse the good aspects of the match, such as our willingness to fight to the last kick of the ball and get a late equaliser. I was still stressing that the aim was only ninth place, anything better than that would be a bonus. The *Sunday Post* remarked that the club finishing above us in the table would be champions! Mind you, Doug Baillie is an ex-Pars player!

There was tremendous pride that young full-back Raymond Sharp was selected for Scotland's under-21 team. He could play at full-back or midfield and had come through the youth and reserve sides. That's the way provincial sides must survive. By the time of the Fir Park game we had also signed Tommy Wilson from St Mirren, so with those two along with Graham Robertson and Jimmy Nicholl I could pick and choose my full-backs according to the opposition and circumstances. Jimmy Nicholl, for example, had received a bad pelvic injury in the Skol Cup-tie with Hibs and would not return till January, a tribute to the work of Pip Yeates who is as useful to us as he is working with the injured actors on Steven Spielberg films.

Any fears that we were in danger of becoming over-confident were halted by successive 0-3 defeats by Aberdeen and Rangers. I want Dunfermline fans one day to enjoy being at or near the top of the League but at that time they were suffering from delusions of grandeur. It was always going to be the usual tough game against

Aberdeen and so it proved. Don's signing Hans Gillhaus had a blinder while Snelders, Nicholas, Bett and McLeish were superb as always. Aberdeen were the best team to play at East End in 1989-90 and that may have been their best performance. They had good balance and exceptional players. Dunfermline's day will come, though.

The fans kept their spirits up, they knew we were doing our best. When Hibs were due in early December I thought Alex Miller was pulling a fast one as we kept hearing the media reports that Andy Goram was injured and wasn't going to make it. Were we being deluded into a false sense of security, I wondered? I had known they had a competent understudy in Chris Reid as I had seen him play as a youngster. However, I felt that, if he played, here was a great chance if ever there was one to defeat Hibs at home. Bookies, being the astute businessmen they are, would never have bet on the performance the boy put up on his debut. Dunfermline played really well but he had three breathtakingly brilliant saves – one of which was so outstanding that George O'Boyle could only shake his head in disbelief and then join with the fans in applauding!

Iain Munro had now become my co-manager and the club was relieved that he was still with us as a number of other clubs had expressed interest in him as manager. I stated in the programme that he was a first-rate coach and I remained ultimately in charge. About the same time the umbrella organisation the Federation of Dunfermline Supporters Clubs began and it was to be more significant than I could ever have dreamed possible.

Having threatened to overrun Hibs, the following Saturday's 0-2 defeat at the hands of Hearts was a disappointment. There was no doubting how big a contribution to the League the club was making. The average gate that Christmas was 11,819 and we had been watched by 94,550 compared to 79,687 in the same period two years earlier. Hamilton had got nowhere near that figure in the whole of their ill-fated Premier season. Attendances had to be reduced, though, to a maximum of 20,164 as a result of the Taylor report, although after £250,000 had been spent on the terracing it had been anticipated that maximum gates of 23,090 would help refund the cash. Since then the maximum attendance has been further reduced by the introduction of the seated family enclosures, an excellent concept.

Christmas was a happy time. The best moment to see your team score a goal is in the dying seconds and that is precisely what Istvan Kozma contrived to do on Boxing Day against Dundee. It was an absolutely vital score in retrospect because it took us an astonishing eight points clear of them with a game in hand. I conceded that no one would have begrudged Dundee a deserved draw but as we celebrated I felt some of the pressure evaporating at last. We had again taken nine points from the second quarter and had 18 points from the 18 games. We were halfway there. I had kept telling the players only to look forward and it was working.

It is hardly surprising that the lads were all fired up for the last game of the decade at Celtic Park. Their performance was incredible, one of the best from the start to finish in the last 20 years and that is no exaggeration. Again I had told them the pressure would all be on Celtic who were not at their best. We had not won there since that fantastic Cup victory in 1968 when they were European Champions and we were on the way to our second Cup win! *Scotland on Sunday* remarked on our impudence for daring to go there and have three foraging attackers! The *Sunday Times* stated that our tactical awareness and breathtaking level of fitness made up for any lack of individual quality. Not too many teams beat Celtic 0-2 on their own bit of turf.

January was a huge contrast with three league defeats which hammered the small squad hit by injury and suspension, yet the team actually played well in the 4-1 defeat at Pittodrie. The 5-0 defeat by Motherwell was the best that any team played against us all season. We were out-played, out-shot, out-thought and out-classed by the team most similar to us in the division. They were excellent that day.

The goals for Ross Jack had dried up and despite brilliant displays George O'Boyle had yet to net one. That was about to change! Some of our best memories are in the Cup and the draw against Hamilton took our minds off the League for the moment. I always knew that a team relegated from the Premier Division would make life tough for us and so it proved. The first game at home was poor. Hamilton had nothing to lose and my old friend John Lambie made sure his team gave a good account of themselves. In the second game I knew that as favourites we would be pressurised and we made sure that we dominated most of the game. The goal by George O'Boyle was a great relief – he scored a handful after that – and we held on with some of the pressure off.

That meant a derby game with near neighbours Cowdenbeath in the next round albeit at Stark's Park, Kirkcaldy. They might only have been Second Division but I personally watched them in three games and assessed their strenghts and weaknesses, got to know their system and players. I told the lads on what was a freezing evening to keep the ball moving at speed and not allow Cowdenbeath to settle or play to their strengths. It was a typical Cup-tie. Cowdenbeath played way above themselves but they had no real answer to the intricate ball skills of Kozma and O'Boyle. The leg break that George suffered at the end, just as we were considering taking him off, was an absolute tragedgy for both the boy and the club and I was disgusted by the abuse hurled at him by both Cowdenbeath and neutral so-called supporters. The memory came back to me of the day I was stretchered off against Hearts when some of their contingent began to sing "You'll never walk again". To his credit and despite the pain, George sat up on the stretcher to acknowledge the applause of our fans.

We prepared meticulously at Dunkeld House Hotel and then Airth Castle for the Celtic Cup game. By coincidence the game was to take place on the same day as Scotland's rugby team were to take on the might of England for the Calcutta Cup, Triple Crown, Five Nations Championship and the Grand Slam. I was inspired by the muse to pen a suitable verse:

> Both teams want to do us proud, so get behind them and sing out loud,
> Captain McCathie and captain Sole, both men plan to play a key role,
> One ball oval, one ball round, let's grind the opposition into the ground,
> Come on ye Pars, come on ye Blues, our town, your country don't want you to lose,
> Walk on to the park, hold your heads up high, this is the day we do or die.

I've often wondered whether the Scottish Rugby XV read my lines! But unfortunately their magnificent triumph on the day was not to be matched by a Pars victory, though we came so close and only a truly magnificent instinctive save by Pat Bonner from Ross Jack near the end prevented us from another semi-final appearance. It was always going to be difficult facing the volume of noise a 41,000 crowd produces at the replay, and so it proved. We were deservedly beaten.

The third quarter of the league programme had ended in early March and we had taken a further eight points. That period included another important 1-0 win over St Mirren which did something to take our minds off our worst game of the season at Love Street as well as a home 0-1 defeat by Rangers when we had two goals disallowed! The important goal against St Mirren was scored by George O'Boyle, who was now on something of a run. He played magnificently in a second win over Hearts, this time 0-2 at Tynecastle. O'Boyle's play was characterised by skill and vision and it was only a fitting conclusion when he strode away from Levein to get the goal which clinched it. Ian Westwater was as inspired as he had been in the league game at Parkhead.

Defeats by Hibs and Aberdeen, inspired by Willie Miller's return, were disappointing. However, by March injury and suspension were taking their toll and one Pars programme asked, "Anyone fancy a game?" There was a further problem. Dundee, who had always been scoring a lot of goals but were conceding even more, were beginning to get their act together, led by the example of born-again Jim Duffy. A blue shadow began to hang ominously over Love Street and East End. The gap began to close. We lost 1-0 at Dundee after four consecutive wins against them. Ian Westwater had a string of impressive saves but Dundee, to their credit, harnessed a strong wind to good effect when conditions made it difficult for the skilful players.

By the time we played Dundee United at the end of the month it was actually a novelty to be preparing the lads for a match other than against Celtic and I said so in the programme. I felt it would be to our advantage that their minds would be on their forthcoming Cup semi-final with Aberdeen but we were sunk by a late goal. Judging by the reaction of the fans the final pass may have been handled towards the striker. However, now the players responded magnificently and a 3-1 win at Motherwell and 2-1 win at St Mirren meant we were safe. The experience and determination of Jimmy Nicholl were a major factor at this time and Kozma's class at Fir Park, against a team which had thrashed us so convincingly last time out, was another important factor – he had a part in all three goals. Westwater had a fine game again. The results showed a lot of character and Ross Jack did well to score two penalties under such pressure.

In between there was another home defeat at the hands of Hearts. George O'Boyle made an all too brief comeback against St Mirren and scored a crucial penalty and with the defence secure until the final moments, Jack's goal wrapped it all up. It was important as Dundee were doing well at Parkhead but must have been heart-broken to hear our half time score. The fans went home singing and Dunfermline, who had had to fight and scratch all the way, had proved the pundits wrong.

We probably surprised many people in the last handful of games when we brought in Sandy Clark but Ross Jack had had a lean spell and George O'Boyle was injured. Sandy was never going to reach the heights of old but he had seen it all and done it all, he was great in training, helped take some of the pressure off and pulled us through in the end.

The players and I celebrated with a meal and I had a tremendous feeling of both pride and satisfaction at what had been achieved. We only finished five points adrift of a place in Europe. We had taken six points off both Dundee and St Mirren when it had been our failure to take points off lowly clubs in 1987-88 that had been our undoing ultimately. We had learned a lot from that experience. Taking a remarkable five points from Celtic and four from Hearts had been a bonus. There had been no real fear of players being snapped up. It had been a transitional period, a period of learning. In fact I believe the club is still probably two years away yet from really challenging for honours, but we did have two great Cup runs and had come eighth, one place higher up the ladder than we had hoped for. The fans went home happy after the last home game with Hibs and they could look forward to the World Cup and then our next campaign.

The title *Survival Special* which appeared on the programme that day was not just a clever comparison with the television programme of the same name. You see, I had always used the word "survival" to avoid talk of dodging relegation – a psychologist to the last, eh! The final attendance came to 212,211 at East End, the fifth highest in Scotland. The supporters had clearly appreciated our efforts.

Chapter 8

THE ROLE OF THE MANAGER

A TRIBUTE TO THE LATE JOCK STEIN
(THEY SHALL NOT FORGET)

The silence over victory was there to be seen
When the news was announced of the death of Jock Stein
Cardiff was stilled with disbelief
As triumph gave way to common grief

Stunned were the fans who, a moment before
Had given way to a victorious roar
Remorse and regret was on each man's face
At the passing of Jock from our earthly race

Never had an army got such a shock
As this tartan army that idolised Jock
On each player's face was that look of sorrow
Of knowing their boss would have no tomorrow

Now there's just memories of this greatest of all
Glorious moments of sweet recall
This statesman of football who led the field
Like his Lisbon Lions who would never yield

In 1967, he performed a feat
With Glasgow Celtic that will never be beat
They won every trophy and competition
Of which there will be no repetition

But his greatest moment when he shook them up
Was that day in Lisbon in the European Cup
Great was his joy in that glorious hour
His pinnacle of fame – for such was his power

Dunfermline will bow their heads in prayer
For once he had them in his care
He took them to Hampden of great renown
And brought the Scottish Cup back to Dunfermline town

All Scotland mourns with many millions more
This immortal manager, we'll always adore
In life he was great, in death we'll remember
That tragic night on the 10th of September

So it's fare ye well Jock, you are Scotland's great loss
To the fans and the players you were always the boss
Yours is the greatest story of them all
Till that night you answered our Saviour's call

From Pars supporters

FOOTBALL is cliché-ridden, and one old chestnut that you always hear managers saying is that they want their players "to play for their shirt". Well, let me tell you about an incident that sums up neatly my feelings for the club. One day, when I was reserve coach, manager Tam Forsyth blasted striker Grant Jenkins, who was having a poor game. Grant was clearly upset and, as he entered the dressing-room, he pulled off his jersey and threw it on the floor. "Pick that up right now," I roared. "That isn't any old jersey, it's a Dunfermline Athletic jersey and don't you ever do that again!" You see, the club means everything to me and one of my first team talks in 1983 was devoted to the honour players should feel when they pull it on.

Anyone who had no pride in wearing it was of no interest to me. Many fans, because of my media image, see me probably as a larger than life character. They know I tell funny stories, write daft poems, they've heard my one-liners and my dressing-room chats have become the stuff legends are made of; but being manager of any club is a serious business and that was the case at Dunfermline. Being a football manager is an extremely insecure occupation. Players win matches but it's the manager who's blamed for the defeat.

Courtesy of Harry Goodwin

We're going the right way, lads

A manager who is too popular and lacks discipline is probably heading for the chop. At Dunfermline I could be one of the lads and many players have become life-long friends. I would share a laugh or joke, but the players also knew that with me the buck stopped. I picked the team; I treated each and every player with respect; I never bore a grudge; I have never talked down to anyone in my managerial career; and I hired and fired. Perhaps my relationship with the players was virtually unique in Scotland but no one can deny that it bore fruit. As you leave the home dressing-room you see the letters DAFC – I told the players they stand for determination, attitude, financial reward and commitment. In small print it reads "Do your all for the club!" That is what I expect of myself and I demanded the same standards from my players. Scottish football is littered with managers who were well liked and unsuccessful. I believe I struck the right balance between popularity and respect and that was to lead to success.

What then is the role of the manager? It's worth answering because it became an issue at the time I left East End. Well, the first

135

task is to appoint an excellent number two. It's a decision I have made twice. First I was torn between Gregor Abel and Alex Kinninmonth, the second time between Iain Munro and my friend Ian Campbell. Alex was ruled out as he was already at Raith Rovers while Ian had too good a job with C. R. Smith and naturally had to think of his family's long-term security. Both Gregor Abel and Iain Munro were to contribute a great deal to two Championship successes and promotion, both being excellent coaches.

I had played against Gregor on a few occasions when he was with Falkirk and then Clydebank, and with the latter he had been with the first club to go from Division Two to the Premier League in 12 months. He also had a Second Division Championship medal with Falkirk, so he knew all about success. I wanted this to rub off. While he was coach at Alloa they too had achieved promotion and he was rewarded when Falkirk took him as assistant manager to Alex Totten. It is history that Alex was snapped up by Rangers so Gregor found himself in the managerial chair for four months. But he didn't enjoy the experience. He felt his strength was in his coaching ability and there was too much administration to be done when he also had a career in teaching. I knew I had to get the man who had made more than 400 appearances with three clubs.

When I was manager of Kelty Hearts, I arranged the club's biggest deal. I sold a player called Andrew Paterson to Alloa and it was then that I met Abel, who greatly impressed me with his handling of the deal. I thought Andrew would do well but, sadly, a bad head and leg injury meant an end to his career. After Gregor resigned, I tried all weekend to get him on the telephone but he was away on an SFA coaching course. When he finally came to East End he discussed for three hours the job and how we would complement each other. Soon things were agreed and we became great friends with a tremendous mutual respect.

He was very much his own man and loved the day-to-day working with players. With him I shared the disappointment of coming third in Division Two, but we also had the excitement of winning the club's first Division Two Championship in 60 years and together we took the club into the Premier League.

Sadly, the club then had to part company with Greg. There is nothing I would have wanted more than to carry on the adventure with him into the Premier League but he had to consider his teaching career at Alva and the security it brought. No club could match that. I would like to put on record my deep gratitude for all that he contributed in Dunfermline's return to the big time. I was moved when Gregor said that his time at East End was the happiest of his football career.

The next partnership would be with Iain Munro and together we would win the First Division Championship and consolidate a year later. Most objective observers felt the partnership therefore worked.

The role of the manager is all about man-management, motivation, encouraging team spirit, identifying strengths and weaknesses and then developing the former while curing the latter. Above all, it is vital to give players the belief that they are better than the opposition and that never changed from playing East Stirling in the early days to playing Rangers at the end of an era. I don't know how often I have told the players, "We are the great Dunfermline Athletic. What right does this team have to think they can come to East End and wipe us off our own park!" I meant every word. At three o'clock on a Saturday afternoon I expected us to beat any team, otherwise I wouldn't have been in the job.

It was important for team spirit to keep the players co-ordinated. I never had any favourites, and my respect for them meant there were never any cliques. If a player was ever dropped I spoke to him individually to explain why and I admit it was easier to do that when the player knew he had played badly rather than when he was playing well but simply did not fit the team pattern. In the latter instance, having to leave Mark Smith out during 1989-90 was awful and I was so pleased when he deservedly moved to Nottingham Forest to further his career. The cavalier style we had employed in 1988-89 in the First Division meant we could afford the luxury of a winger and Mark was ideal with his electric pace, but we simply could not be so adventurous in the Premier.

In the reserves you have up-and-coming youngsters, players returning from injury and players who, for whatever reason, are out of favour in the first team. It depended on the personality of the player how you dealt with their disappointment. Players like Jimmy Nicholl and Doug Rougvie are old pros and know the score. Davie Irons was playing well but was kept out for long periods by Istvan Kozma, while Ray Farningham had a great mental attitude and plugged away in the second team waiting to grab the opportunity which came his way at the end of the season. With Paul Smith and Stuart Rafferty playing so consistently, it was difficult to dispossess them.

I encouraged the team spirit in a variety of ways. There were trips to Powderhall or Gullane, bowling alleys and golf courses. We stayed at St Andrews and Dunblane in top hotels and, like Jock Stein before me, I insisted they travelled to games in a luxurious coach, had the best of meals and achieved a group identity through the club blazers and flannels. The players knew they were being cared for and it was rare for anyone to go over the score. But John Watson was one who did!

We had all gone to Gullane for the day. We trained at a local park, had a coffee and then a round of golf. Back at the hotel we had a meal and then presented our golf prizes, which Bobby Forrest won so often I did wonder about his ability to count! Anyway, on this occasion the lads were given the evening off but were told to be back by midnight. After a couple of drinks Gregor and I went for a walk. As we were passing this hotel we suddenly saw John Watson "mooning" out of the window. I gave him a good kick, I can tell you. He never did it again.

I had no time for yes men at East End. I spent about 40 per cent of my week with the tracksuit on, working with the players, although Gregor and then Iain were in charge of the day-to-day coaching. I had the final decision on the Saturday team sheet but this was after full consultation and discussion with my coach. The procedure at Dunfermline for my seven years of management was to discuss the selection of the team and the tactics with my right hand man. At this time it was Iain Munro. Usually on a Thursday or a Friday we would sit down and decide who would play or who would not play on the Saturday. If there was any doubt or any disagreement I always had the final say. On very few occasions did we disagree on the team. Iain Munro was in sole charge of the coaching, that was his main duty at the club. To my credit, I didn't interfere with him as he was good at his job. Because the club had grown so big and so fast in the previous four years I found it more difficult to always be at the training, but I knew that Iain Munro and my assistants were doing a fine job, and if I wasn't training on particular days – and sometimes I couldn't make it for two days at a time – I knew that the job would be carried out professionally. A manager should delegate duties and when delegating these duties should not interfere in any way. The main decision is to make sure that the person employed is the right man for the job. Equally, I always liaised closely with the reserve manager, latterly Phil Bonnyman, and this was a boost too for the second team players who knew I'd be fully briefed on how they were developing.

I was a manager at only 29 and although I was influenced by George Miller I learned the job as I went along. Naturally I made mistakes. When our First Division campaign began I signed centre-back Grant Reid from Stenhousemuir. When Davie Young was left out of the team there was a major blow-up. Davie demanded to know why he had been dropped and the conversation was decidedly heated. Davie told me I could "shove the club". I showed my fists and the whole thing went over the score. Reid broke his nose soon afterwards, Young was reinstated, had a truly wonderful season and was probably the best centre-back in the division. He had proved me wrong, but in doing so did a great deal for the team. I like proving people wrong too and I ended up with great respect for him.

Players realised from then onwards that I never held a grudge. Sometimes, after a bad result, I would shout, snarl, spit, swear and fume at the team, my face red with anger. I never wanted the team to let down the punters who had parted with their hard-earned cash. The night we went top at Fir Park, when we drew 1-1 with Motherwell, was just such an evening. We'd been awful. But the following morning I called the squad together and we analysed all the good points of the match, like fighting to the end and battling for a late equaliser.

If I gave any player an individual rollicking, I learned that I had to take into account his personality. A case in point was Bobby Forrest, who was a vital player at East End, but who had little confidence. After one 7-2 reserve defeat at Dens Park I really tore into him – he'd had a nightmare. My eyes were popping out of my head in anger. "You should pack it in and go back to gardening," I roared unthinkingly. The following Monday morning he knocked at my office door. "Can I have time off, gaffer, today?" he enquired. "Whatever for?" I replied. "Well, at 12 o'clock I've an interview to get my old nursery job back again." I made my peace in double quick time! A few years later, the day we won the First Division Championship, Bobby was playing for Meadowbank and it was his cross which led to their goal. As their players celebrated, Bobby had his head in his hands. He was a great servant of the club.

A player can have a bad game for a club and usually he knows it and then you must work on his confidence and encourage him. Ian Westwater is normally impeccable but did not have to be told that he had had a poor game in the 0-3 defeat by Aberdeen. Because of the great team spirit I feel I engendered, I never had a player who blamed others for his own mistakes or any who got too big for his boots. They knew they were all cogs in a machine, that all the cogs were of equal size and that each cog was dependent on the next. I did not tolerate any player who tried to "hide" in a game.

Being manager of a provincial club, I had to be very careful in the transfer market. We had to call a board meeting in 1983 to see if we could scrape together £2,000 plus signing-on fee for Allan Forsyth. By 1989 we splashed out £600,000 on Istvan Kozma, albeit in instalments. I was trying to compete with the Old Firm and Aberdeen or Hearts but the cash I had to spend wouldn't have kept Graeme Souness in aftershave. Buying Craig Robertson for £25,000 and selling him to Aberdeen for £173,000 and buying Ian McCall for £7,000 and selling him for £200,000 were crucial deals. In the case of the latter I told the Press I had "sold an ace to buy four kings" and that summed it up.

It was to be the most difficult decision I ever made as a manager to allow players to leave in the autumn of 1987 who had given their all for the club, who had given us the Division Two Championship and then achieved promotion again. I've said repeatedly that I would always be proud to walk down Dunfermline High Street with them and many are still my friends today, I am glad to say. People like Davie Moyes, Jimmy Bowie, Gary Thomson, Bobby Robertson, Davie Young, Grant Jenkins and Bobby Forrest are great guys.

One way of keeping up a good relationship with the players was always to give them time off for such reasons as weddings, funerals and births but once I almost came unstuck there. I knew that Hugh Whyte's wife was almost about to have a baby and that being a doctor he would want to help at the birth. I prayed that it wouldn't coincide with a match day but of course it did! Hugh phoned at eight in the morning to tell me his wife was in labour. We had a vital away game at Cowdenbeath and Ian Westwater was also unavailable, with a broken finger. From eight-thirty to one-thirty I phoned everywhere. My back-up was the reserve goalie at Forfar but he had injured his back. In the end Hill of Beath, who would

Receiving the second Manager of Month Award, but losing to Aberdeen took the joy away, 1 February 1989

later go on to do the district proud in the Junior Cup, said I could borrow their goalkeeper, Dave Westwood, a Pars fanatic who had already had experience with Raith Rovers and Cowdenbeath, for which I will always be indebted to manager Finlayson and his committee. Then there was the problem that we had to help find them cover. Westwood, after a nervous start, went on to have a blinder and we won 0-1. I turned up at the game unshaved, with no tie and in casual clothes – I had been on the phone for hours!

By speaking to players individually, and with some hilarious though relevant team talks, I always did all I could to motivate the team, although in truth if a player isn't motivated to play, say, a Cup-tie with Rangers or Aberdeen in front of a packed crowd then there is something far wrong. In playing these teams it was more important to psyche out the opposition. A case in point was the Cup game with Aberdeen when we were in the First Division. Alex Smith is an outstanding manager but I had a feeling that the Dons players would underestimate us and mentally they might already have the game won, just as Rangers had done a year earlier. That 2-0 win was a warning to Aberdeen so I needed a plan. I took my team to Dunblane Hydro and we worked very hard on our preparations at nearby Stirling University. However, when all the cameras turned up with the press entourage we made a point of being seen relaxing, playing cards or snooker. We wanted to plant that image in the minds of the Dons players and it almost worked. We drew 0-0 at East End and were thwarted by two of the greatest saves I've ever seen, by Theo Snelders from Ross Jack. Those incidents were shown again on screen when both players subsequently took divisional Player of the Year awards.

The difficulty with motivation comes when you play the lesser clubs and that is where a manager's skills will be seen to best light. In August 1989 I bought all the newspapers which were predicting in unison that the Athletic would go straight back down again. I showed them to my squad and that got them angry. Then we spoke about living standards and agreed that we had not gone through all the ups and downs of the Championship to throw it all away now. We agreed that we would be playing in a mini-league, if you like, of Dundee, St Mirren, Motherwell and Hibs and would have to go in for what Bob Crampsey called "damage limitation" against the rest. We beat Dundee in the opening game and unlike Lot's wife – another story I quoted – never looked back. The six points taken from both Dundee and St Mirren proved that the players were motivated. We played a 5-2-1-2 system which was not defensive. We had two attacking full-backs and Kozma, with his magnificent individuality, played all over the park. Add that to the buying of experienced professionals like Rougvie and Nicholl, the consistency of the midfield and class of the two strikers and you have the ingredients for what developed into a successful season.

Part of being a manager is having a good relationship with the media and I think I did. It was vital at first because we needed publicity to get the crowds and without them you can't get the cash to buy better players who in turn attract more fans until the snowball is off down the hill. I only received three phone calls in my first week at East End. I can safely say that when the Press slagged the Pars we probably deserved it and by the same token when they gave lavish praise we'd worked hard to attain that. The *Dunfermline Press* always gave a lot of coverage but as we have grown in stature so the national Press has given us more space too. Mind you, Jim Kean of the *Daily Record* always says I take a hundred sentences to say what I could put across in one! The Press take me as they find me, I've no airs and graces, I am still a Lochgelly boy, born and bred, and they can take it or leave it. One paper wanted an exclusive at the time of my resignation but that would hardly have been fair.

I have mentioned how vital I think it is to maintain high standards and I must admit that on one occasion I let mine slip. When we played Clyde in the second last game of the Division One Championship I genuinely believed that would be the promotion and Championship match. I didn't wear my usual club blazer and flannels but, being a right poser, sat in the dugout with a tracksuit on, all set for the photographs in the papers. In the event we blew it drawing 1-1. I learned later that I was slagged by Stuart Beedie, and he was right. The following week, when we did go up, I was dressed appropriately but thankfully, being superstitious, did not wear my watch. The last few minutes were unbearable enough without one!

Football management, then, is by no means the laugh-a-minute career that my media image seems to have created in some people's minds but there are still some moments of real fun and they are vital in cementing team spirit. The best example of all must be the story behind the making of the Pars theme song *East Enjer* .

In early 1986 the club was going for the Division Two Championship and, with the realisation that the BBC soap *EastEnders* was about to celebrate its first anniversary that February, Blair Morgan, the director, suggested cutting a record of the catchy tune but using words appropriate to the club, which he and his son Stephen would pen. Gregor Abel wrote and sang the 'B' side *The Dunfermline Song* and when we overheard him at the recording studio telling people that his stage name was Greg, we called him that from then on, as well as "The Singing Coach"! At the studios we had some real musicians with us to both sing and play the music and the players and I read the verses off a large sheet of paper. It was later shown on *Reporting Scotland*. As a result we were contacted by *Pebble Mill At One* in Birmingham who wanted us to go down there and perform in a show which would also include Anna Wing from the programme, Magnus Magnusson and Paul Coia. We were delighted and all the players were looking forward to the outing.

The problem was that on the evening we were to go down by coach the BBC phoned me to say we would not be allowed to mime or read off a sheet. We would have to sing it live with no prompting! This meant that the lads would have to get it word-perfect on the bus going down instead of watching a video and relaxing or having a drink. Then came my brain-wave – I hired a really racy porn video and showed it on the coach. Everytime we got to one of the "good bits" which the players were dying to see, I stopped the tape and said I would not re-start it till they had learned the verse. They had the song off by heart in double quick time!

We got to the hotel and we all had a few drinks before turning in. John Watson, however, had a few too many and fell under the table. In the morning he was contrite but I told him he still wasn't taking part "How am I going to explain this to my Mum?" he asked in desperation.

We were at the studios full of anticipation and excitement by nine-thirty, met the producer and stage manageress and did our rehearsals for the next two hours, learning where to stand, where to look, knowing the cue and so on. Eventually came the final rehearsal. The studio was hushed. The classical pianist, who was on before us completed her piece and the stage manageress began the 60-second countdown on her fingers off camera. I was aware of the sound people doing their final checks.

With exactly three seconds to go and the tension excruciating, Stephen Morrison farted loudly. The place collapsed! The pianist frowned, I ran up to Stephen to throttle him and Paul Coia suggested that one of our players must have a sore throat! He's never been allowed to forget it either.

Well, the record did sell 4,000 copies and I was so proud to learn that we had got to number one – in Uganda! I bet they used the records for earrings too!

Daft wee adventures like these all helped foster a wonderful family feeling about the club. That was one of my main aims, just as my charity and social events and ventures like setting up the Centenary Club were to build a marvellous relationship with the community so that the fans always felt we were all equals and everyone was important. People like Danny Hutchinson who did such a fantastic job with the pitch or Andy Young or Joe Nelson or the people doing the laundry were all vital to the club, but one story will explain what I am getting at.

Sandy Bernard has always been around, looking after the boots. It's a real labour of love and you couldn't do without him. One day

Eric Ferguson's winning goal against Celtic, 22 August 1987

Joe Nelson, Mr Handyman

John Watson complained to him that his boots hadn't scored a goal in three weeks! "Couldn't you talk to them, Sandy, and get them to respond?" John suggested, laughing. The following day John and Norrie McCathie were going towards the sponsors' lounge when they heard Sandy's voice in the bootroom. "Come on, you daft boots," he was saying. "For Gods's sake score for John!" Sandy really is quite a character. Before the Rangers Cup game we asked him up to the hotel in St Andrews as he's such a loyal club servant. Ken McNaught and I drove up to collect him with the car boot crammed with golf clubs and suitcases. Sandy had an Asda bag with only his pyjamas and toilet bag! That wasn't all. Later that week he took me proudly to a pub to meet his cronies. He was the youngest there – and he's in his early seventies!

I believe, then, that our phenomenal success has been due to the balance I have struck between being the right b****** who swears, shouts, cajoles and bawls at players and someone the players have to regard, if not as a friend, then as someone they can respect. If I can be criticised for pushing anyone too far then I have not pushed anyone harder than I would push myself. I have learned lessons, I have made mistakes but the bottom line is that there was no one to manage Jim Leishman. Dunfermline Athletic's success is due to dedication and a lot of damn hard work with everyone pulling together for the club, and the players have been rewarded with bigger crowds and a larger pay packet. Our playing system worked but it still allowed for individuality and flair.

Dunfermline is a big club now, a club that has brought a lot of the fun back to Scottish football. Who is to say where we might have ended up together?

Chapter 9

DUNFERMLINE STARS

I've had more time to think about my manager's role
Now that I am unemployed and on the dole
Sitting in the house with John writing this book
being on the outside, peering in, having a look
Taking account of the mistakes and triumphs over the years
Looking back with no regrets and having no fears

Having great memories of some great men
And achieving our goal of reaching the top ten
Being the manager for me was a great feat
And I'm sure my record will be hard to beat

You Scottish supporters, don't you slack
Because make no mistake, Big Jim will be back
Maybe not this month, next month or next year
But sometime in the future, don't you fear!

EVERY generation throws up a hero. People like Charlie Dickson,
Roy Barry and Alex Ferguson. Well there is no disputing who was
the greatest hero at East End in recent years. "John, John, super
John," the fans used to shout if the opposition were giving John
Watson stick and that probably sums him up. I signed him late in
1983 and no manager anywhere ever did a better deal. Even the
transfer was strange. He had been playing in Hong Kong for the
local Rangers, where he could also work as a plumber, but he
hadn't settled and now he was back in Scotland. On the recommen-
dation of Andy Young, I went across to Edinburgh to meet him in
the Café Royal but the place was mobbed. We found somewhere

Courtesy of Dunfermline Athletic Football Club

John Watson, a true great

quieter and there I negotiated the transfer for £300, plus one pint of Special for John and a pint of Guinness for his girlfriend!

There was no suggestion then that he would become the vital player of subsequent years, in fact he was at least a stone overweight and out of condition. But John's whole career is like something out of a children's comic. Unlike so many players who have schoolboy caps, John hardly ever played football in his teens. Instead, as a pupil at Liberton High he preferred to support Hibs on Saturday afternoons. When he did get round to playing football he was in Division Seven of the Edinburgh Amateur League – and that was in goal! Willie McFarlane took him to Meadowbank where he had two undistinguished seasons – incredibly without scoring once. He moved back to the Amateur League and he eventually ended up in Hong Kong.

Even when he was first with us there was nothing really to suggest that he was going to end up the kids' greatest hero since Fergie. He used to score regularly in the reserves but he played 17 times in the first team before he scored, ending up with only three by the end of the season. Then the goals started to flow. He scored 18 in 1984 and I was delighted when he was honoured with the Scottish Brewers Player of the Month Award – such awards rarely came East End's way in those days!

One of my proudest moments at East End in my seven years came the night when John scored his 30th goal of the season against St Johnstone to clinch the *Daily Record's* Golden Shot trophy to go along with his Championship medal. When he scored his 31st he proved to be our greatest scorer since Fergie. His grand total already came to 50 and only Sandy McNaughton had achieved that feat in the previous 20 years. After that there was great pleasure when, like Norrie McCathie, he was capped for the Scotland semi-professional team. He also took a succession of Man of the Match awards and Player of the Year trophies.

In the First Division he remained the club's top goalscorer with 13 goals despite the much tighter marking, and he always made a tremendous contribution despite injuries. John scored a further 20 goals, bringing his tally to 85 – not a bad return on my investment of £300!

At the beginning of 1989-90 John was in the team photograph for our first season back in the Premier Division but he decided to leave. I had told him that he could not expect to make as many appearances at that level and John said, "Well, I'd rather be remembered by the fans when I was at the top, boss." There was no better way for him to end his career with the club than his scoring the equalising goal against Meadowbank which gave us the Championship.

"BIGGER THAN BIG JIM!"

That's the big range of furnishings at Landmark's new Dunfermline superstore.

Landmark has always been big in this area. Now, with our new superstore in Dunfermline we're getting even bigger. Not so big that you'll be worn out just walking round — but big enough to house the best display of furnishings in town.

BIG CHOICE

Unlike some of the "furniture barns" you've seen, we don't display our entire stock. We display just one of everything — but can give you virtually immediate delivery on a huge range from our massive central warehouse.

BIG NAMES

You'll find we don't just have a big range of suites, beds, carpets, dining and bedroom furniture at Landmark.

NOW OPEN

Halbeath

Retail Park,

Dunfermline.

landmark
Home Furnishing
OPEN 7 DAYS

you should see what we're up to!

We've got all the big names too: Cintique, Coloroll, Ducal, McIntosh, Axminster, Ege, Kossett, Sealy, Silentnight and many, many more.

BIG VALUE

But just because we're big on quality, doesn't mean you have to pay big prices. All our furnishings are carefully selected to give you the best possible value for money — no matter what your price range.

BIG WELCOME

So, visit our new superstore at the Halbeath Retail Park this weekend — and see what we're up to. You're sure of a big, big welcome.

PRE-CHRISTMAS DELIVERY FROM STOCK.

Clydebank · Cowcaddens · Dundee · Dunfermline · Edinburgh · Stirling · Uddingston

Landmark used this full-page advert in the Dunfermline Press *to launch the opening of their new store in Halbeath Retail Park, Dunfermline, in December 1989*

John was a great character and I watched him turn into a Pars fan himself. He never let the supporters down at any function, he spent ages with kids and promoted the club like the true professional he is. A lot of the adventures I talk about in the book centre on him. His strength, long red hair and towering height made him easily identifiable and as the cameras came, so he became a real celebrity. He was one of the best headers of the ball I have ever seen. His goals varied from the ludicrous (John called his goal against Ayr the best slice since he last played golf) to the brilliant (the flying header from a Beedie corner and a Mark Smith flick on which put Rangers out of the Cup). He was as fearless as his racing driver namesake and could cause chaos in the opposition box, finishing off crosses from Jim Bowie and building up an uncanny understanding with Ian Campbell and later Ross Jack, the First Division Player of the Year. He was also versatile and before we signed Grant Tierney he did a great job in central defence. There are many reasons why we soared from obscurity but John, the plumber who could plug a leaky defence and supply goals on tap, was always a major factor.

Norrie McCathie was another stalwart during the Leishman era. He and his pal John Watson now run Cagney's Pub in the town, where we celebrated the First Division Championship in style! I didn't sign him, I inherited him. He had come to the Pars back in 1981 from Cowdenbeath. Norrie was playing in midfield then and he was quite a goal scorer. He had notched up 38 by the time I left, 22 of them by 1985 when I decided to put him in the back four. He had great strength in the opposition box but I felt his contribution over the 90 minutes was not sufficient and his passing could have been more accurate. It was a time when we were losing far too many silly goals so I moved him to shake up the defence.

Players who have played with him like Grant Reid, Davie Young and Grant Tierney told me later that they had played the best football of their careers beside him. He was one of the strongest players and best tacklers Dunfermline ever had and perhaps the most underestimated. He always fought to the last minute, as his equaliser at Forfar in a 3-3 game and incredible last gasp winner in a 1-0 thriller at Clyde proved. On that second occasion he won the ball in his own box, interpassed to the halfway line, took on the Clyde defence and stabbed it home.

I used to keep telling him I made him one of the best centre-backs ever – "I taught you everything!" On the day I resigned I exchanged a few personal words and then I watched, misty-eyed, as the Pars minibus drove off without me to the training ground. Norrie popped his head out of the window and shouted, "I told you I'd see you out the door!"

Lots of clubs took an interest but I would never let him go and no one deserved a Testimonial more than he. I was determined to see the match in his honour too, even if in disguise and a false beard! Like John he is a hero among the fans and the strong-tackling, rugged defender also gave unselfishly of his time to charity and social occasions. Like John, he'll be a fan long after he has stopped playing.

If I had a second best signing then it was "Westy". Ian Westwater was signed for only £3,500 from Hearts in the spring of 1985. I wanted a young, talented goalkeeper who would eventually take over from Hugh Whyte who, as a doctor, had professional commitments. We saw Ian against Morton Reserves and were very impressed. He had just the right pedigree; a father who himself had been a goalkeeper, a host of schoolboy caps and Scottish professional caps, and the honour of being the youngest player to play in goal in the Premier Division. My faith in him has been repaid as his numerous shutouts (a dozen last season in the Premier League) bear testimony.

Ian is acrobatic, incredibly brave, speaks non-stop to his defence (you could hear him above the crowd at Ibrox and Parkhead), makes fantastic instinctive saves, has excellent organisational abilities, has perfected the art of taking a cross ball and is always superfit. His Player of the Match and Player of the Year awards were hugely deserved. He was mightily relieved when we won the League in 1989 because the goal we lost to Clyde the previous week when he walked back across the line clutching the ball to give them the equaliser would otherwise have lived with him forever. That would have been unfair as we should have lost 1-3 but for him that day. His save in the 2-1 home win over Celtic from Andy Walker was perhaps the greatest I have ever witnessed.

If it hadn't been for the fact that he was overshadowed by John Watson, fans might be more aware of the mighty contribution made by my pal, Ian Campbell. Ian, of course, was at the club as a player from 1973 to 1975, at the same time as me, but when the club went part-time he was freed and he eventually signed for

Brechin. Brechin then had one of their most successful periods, winning the Second Division Championship in 1983. I brought him back to Dunfermline in the Spring of 1985, all set for the following year's assault on that same flag.

I've said before that he would have been my first choice as coach when we reached the dizzy heights of the Premier Division. Mind you, the only mistake I made in the difficult negotiations with Brechin boss Ian Fleming (who wouldn't budge an inch on the transfer fee he wanted) was that I thought I was buying Dick – well, I never could tell the two of them apart! In the end there was a player swap as well, with John Perry leaving.

I had always resisted the idea of surrounding myself, as some managers do, with their personal friends but Ian just had to be the exception. He was a proven goal scorer who would go on to nab 18 for us in 1985-86. He was one of the best finishers in Divisions One and Two and he complemented John Watson superbly. He later became player-coach. His ideas and insights were a tremendous boon to the club. I'll never forgive him, though, for one comment he made to the media. "How does Dunfermline compare now to the club of the 1970s?" he was asked? "Well, Jim Leishman looks like my Grandad," he replied!

Jim Bowie was a complete nutter but no one was more popular among the supporters and John Watson, who depended so much on him for his accurate crosses at free kicks, was as furious as the fans when he left in March 1987. Suffice to say that I valued him so highly that I rated him the best crosser of a ball since Alex Edwards and I cannot pay him a higher compliment than that. He had been with the club as far back as the days of manager Harry Melrose and made more than 200 appearances for us. Everyone, I think, will remember the story of how "Ziggy", as he was called, once stopped a promising move against Queen of the South when, most unusually, a player had collapsed with hypothermia! He was a real gentleman on the park.

One of the greatest goals he ever made was against Montrose, who used to play an effective defensive five against us. He sent in a perfectly flighted ball which the diving Watson finished in glorious style. He also made a vital contribution to the Second Division Championship year.

On one occasion I felt I treated him badly and I always regret it. We were playing away to Dumbarton and I had decided to leave

154

Courtesy of Dunfermline Athletic Football Club

Bobby Robertson, one of Dumfermline's greatest captains, receiving his award for the record number of appearances, from Chairman Mel Rennie

him on the bench. Through no fault of his own, he arrived ten minutes late so I had amended the team sheet. I gave him a row and said he was not in the first eleven because of his lateness. Certainly I had to set an example to the players but deep down I felt really bad about it. If Mark Smith had had his ability to cross a ball, he would have been dynamite.

I cannot think of Bobby Robertson without my mind drifting back to the day when the Leishman era began. Back in 1983 I was on a coach sitting beside Bobby as we returned from a reserve game at Dumbarton. Things seemed to be at rock bottom. I was reserve coach trying to rebuild my football career so savagely ended as a player and Bobby was trying to give time and commitment both to his job as a junior hospital doctor and to the football club he loved.

155

The team was stuck wretchedly near the foot of Division Two, the players' morale was shattered and there was so little atmosphere at East End that they could have used the place to train astronauts for Mars. I've no recollection of that evening's game but I remember the passion with which Bobby and I recalled the great days of the 1960s. We discussed why things had hit rock bottom and, with ludicrous optimism, discussed the future. I was hardly to know that six weeks later I would be in the hot seat.

No one was more dedicated as a player or more loyal as a fan than Bobby and he was so proud to hold the Second Division Championship trophy and then to take the club into the Premier Division when so many other captains had failed. From the start I told him, tongue in cheek, that I would make him the best right-back since I played. In fact he developed into the most consistent right-back I have ever seen and he deserved his Player of the Year Award. He was a great man-marker and whenever other teams did play a winger against us, he would simply cut off their supply of dangerous crosses. He inspired his mates and he could be my only choice for club captain. Because of his job he usually had to train on his own and I knew that I could depend on him. He was always really fit.

Sometimes I would use Bobby and Ian Campbell as guinea pigs for my team talks, ushering them into my office and briefing them on what to reply when I spoke to the other players in the dressing-room. Sometimes Bobby, for devilment, would not respond in the way he had been primed. I recall I was going to give a talk on how much I disliked yes men, so I asked him to say yes to everything I asked. Of course he kept answering in the negative and it brought the house down. No one was more loyal than Bobby, who told me his favourite playing partner was Bonar Mercer, and no one played more games for the Pars. He was to wear eight different jerseys for us – but not at the same time I hasten to add!

One of the most devastating players at East End and a player we were delighted to get back in 1990 was Ian McCall, whom all the fans called "Diego"! Incredibly, we were to get him for a mere £7,000. He was a player with Queen's Park and he always caused us trouble. In fact I think he scored in all but one game against us! I have great admiration for the Hampden coach Eddie Hunter, who has the love affair with Queen's Park that I have with Dunfermline. It must be soul-destroying to see all your best players disappear at

156

Ian McCall is Tarzan, Norrie McCathie is D'Artagnan, John Watson, the hairy fairy, Rowan Hamilton is King Henry, Eric Ferguson . . . and the daddy of them all is Santa

the end of each and every season but, to his eternal credit, Eddie then unearths more precious talent and along come the big clubs again. Eddie's undying love for Hampden is the main reason he has never been tempted away. He must have been pleased with the way he handled the transfer because he later put us on to Mark Smith and Paul O'Brien.

Ian signed in May 1986 and scored eight goals in our promotion year. His asthma did not in any way hinder him in his dazzling displays in midfield, setting up moves, sometimes finishing them off and always prompting with the accurate flicks and crosses that became his trademark and led to his nickname, which could not be more apt.

At the start of the 1987-88 season he was in devastating form in the 2-1 defeat of Celtic and then the 1-4 Skol Cup defeat by

157

Rangers. We had taken five out of eight points and it had not gone unnoticed that he had been a major factor. Graeme Souness wanted a replacement for the ageing Davie Cooper and he phoned up with an offer. Ian was informed but didn't want to go, rather like Ken Mackie all those years ago. His initial reaction was that he was happy with his postion at East End where he was almost guaranteed first team football, while the same might not be the case at Ibrox. The fee went up, Ian said no again. Finally it reached £200,000 and Ian, faced with the prospect of working with people like Souness and Smith, playing with top professionals before huge crowds and furthering his career, finally agreed. It is perhaps relevant to state here that religion was never mentioned throughout the negotiations. A few days later he was on the Rangers bench against Celtic and we had the cash to go out and buy some much-needed players. A section of the fans did not see it that way and at our next game against Dundee at Dens Park the personal abuse directed at me was so bad that my mother who was there supporting the team felt she had to leave at half time. The fans felt I had sold them down the river and I found that hard to take as I believed I had done the best for the club and the player.

I was really sad that it did not work out for Ian at Ibrox where he only made a few appearances but scored a tremendous goal against Hibs. He has great potential, he has a wonderful talent and he works hard at his game. He will never be a clone. We simply couldn't afford to move for him when he was transferred from Ibrox to Bradford although naturally we did enquire. We got him back at a steal of £100,000 later and the fans have yet to see him at his peak. His greatest strength is making other players feel the same pride in wearing the jersey that I had felt. He also became a Pars fan who watched our games on occasions even when he was a Rangers player. He feels the East End atmosphere is unique but no one has been more of a thorn in my flesh or has given me more sleepless nights!

Talk of big money transfers brings me neatly to Craig Robertson. What an asset to the club he turned out to be and yet he was only with us for 18 months. When I first worked out the deal with Raith Rovers for £25,000 my board was not totally convinced but I had to hand it to them for their faith in my judgement. "You are in charge," they told me. The directors never interfered and allowed me to stand or fall by my record.

Who's that – Diego?

Craig is one of the nicest people you could ever hope to meet. He was a tremendous threat in midfield and had a knack of ghosting into the box like Martin Peters. He was to make 63 appearances in a black and white jersey and would score 19 goals, but what gave us so much pride in the 1987-88 Premier season was that he would end up as the highest midfield scorer in the division, yet as a team we had been struggling. It spoke volumes for him to end up ahead of the likes of Paul McStay. St Mirren's Tony Fitzpatrick, who has always impressed me, tried to entice him to Love Street and Dundee were another club which enquired but Aberdeen, a top club with European ambitions and top internationalists, also became interested in Craig and eventually took him to Pittodrie for £175,000.

I wanted Craig to stay but knew the Pars could get two good players with the money. On the drive to Aberdeen I was unwell and stopped in Stonehaven for a cough bottle. The media tale that I stopped the car to offer Craig more cash to stay at East End Park has no substance in fact. He scored at Pittodrie within 20 minutes of his debut. As with Ian McCall, though, I would have loved to bring Craig back. When there was press speculation that Aberdeen were interested in our talented youngster Ray Sharp I briefly thought it might happen.

About the same time, John Holt left. He made more than 50 appearances and was one of the "four kings" I had bought with the Ian McCall cash. He was unhappy with Division One football but while he was with us in the Premier Leauge he had displayed all the skill and consistency of old and became a Player of the Year.

Writing this chapter has brought back many happy memories of a glorious seven years in my time at East End, yet they would include probably the saddest moment of my life. I am referring to the tragic death of that fine young athlete Gary Riddell.

I had signed Gary in September 1987. I had been searching by and large for experienced campaigners who could keep us in the Premier League and it probably surprised many when I moved for a young reserve centre-back who hadn't even played in Aberdeen's first team. He played well both that season and in the subsequent Championship year and was such a vital component in our success. He was bitterly disappointed, I know, at being left out of the team for the last game of the Championship season against Meadowbank but he took my decision with dignity. No one enjoyed the celebrations more than Gary.

Courtesy of Dunfermline Athletic Football Club

Craig Robertson, Scotland's top-scoring mid-fielder, season 1987/88

He was always out assisting with charity events, helping youngsters or visiting primary schools. He was deeply moved by the Hillsborough tragedy and decided to take part in the famous Dunfermline half-marathon to raise sponsorship for the appeal.

I was already in Florida on holiday when the phone call came with the news of his premature death during that event. I was utterly devastated, and then frustrated that I couldn't get a flight back in time for the funeral. I ended up having a private service at exactly the same moment at a local Catholic Chapel and, although a life-long Protestant, I felt I just had to light a candle for him.

It kept flooding back back to me that the last time I had spoken to him we had got into a heated argument over his new contract and he slammed the door. I felt gutted.

Later, at the memorial service at East End, I had intended speaking for five minutes but I looked up at Gary's mother crying in the stand and I just had to stop. I had meant to say that he is now with God, someone who will always listen to him, someone who will have faith in him and who will always look after him. He had died trying, as usual, to help others. He will never be forgotten.

I brought Stuart Beedie to the club in March 1987 and understood it would be a bit of a risk because of his injury record. But I knew that he had become unhappy at Hibs and that he had had an oustanding career with St Johnstone and Dundee United. His main strength was his quite remarkable acceleration. He would seemingly go from a trot and a jog to a full sprint in a split second. Who can forget the goal against Hibs at home when he burst down the left wing and hit that immaculate cross for Craig Robertson to score? He was also phenomenally accurate with corner kicks or set pieces.

We used to have the occasional set-tos and almost came to blows after we had played badly but beaten Meadowbank away 1-0. However, we had a great mutual respect. Injury curtailed Stuart's appearances but I know many fans argue that he was the most influential midfielder of that period. I was sorry when he left to go to Dundee, and how typical of him to score against us in the opening game! We had the last laugh that day, though.

Also from the Easter Road club came Bobby Smith, and his vast experience of playing at the top level in Scotland and England was a real asset. He was classed as a veteran at 35 but gave us a great two years and he was a wonderful captain in our Championship year.

Another who brought similar experience was the unforgettable "Jaws" himself – Doug Rougvie. We needed such a player for just one season and his sister, who lives just two doors up from me in Keltybridge, told me he wanted to return to Scotland. If Dunfermline had been a big club in the 1970s and early 1980s players of the calibre of Connelly, Malpas and Rougvie would

Courtesy of Dunfermline Athletic Football Club

Sadly missed but never forgotten, Gary Riddell, who died on 11 June 1989, just 29 days after the club took the Championship

never have passed us by. Indeed big Doug actually played for the Dunfermline Youth team as a raw youngster! Anyway, he gave us a great year and had a near unique relationship with the fans. His long throws were unforgettable and he hit that wonderful goal against Hibs in the Skol Cup, which was an inspiration to others. The respect and love for the man was evident in the applause he gained when we met the Dons! He had seen it all, had Doug. It's hard to quantify just how much he did for us in keeping us up last season and then, when it was all over, he thanked us and left.

You need people in a team who are an inspiration and who are always guaranteed to give their all. Take Davie Moyes who was the Alf Tupper of Dunfermline Athletic! He signed in March 1983 and had to make his debut that same evening against East Stirling. I met him on a building site, convinced him to sign and he rushed to the ground in his overalls. The players got stripped and I began my team talk in the dressing-room. Suddenly I realised I was one man short. I found him in the kitchen having a Scotch pie! I ended up on the pitch just before kick-off trying frantically to explain the team formation and tactics! Dave, though, played a vital role in our championship team.

Gary Thompson was a similar competitor and, like Ian McCall, he had always performed creditably against us, in his case with both Alloa and Falkirk. He could play a bit, never got mucked about, led by example and his extra bite really helped our promotion challenge in 1987.

If we did have a Platini at East End then only Stephen Morrison could have had that title. Before he went to Hamilton he was our longest serving player, having been signed by Pat Stanton. He was a striker when he came from Aberdeen and scored 48 for us but I converted him into an efficient midfielder. He was a regular player who became a firm favourite with the crowd and he won the Mr Superfit award in the famous Cup-tie at Ibrox. His shooting power first developed under Alex Ferguson at St Mirren.

You really see how far I brought the club when you begin comparing the transfer fees of these key players in our campaigns. It's hard to imagine now that it took two weeks of board meetings and arguments to free the £2,000 plus the signing-on fee I required for Alan Forsyth of Raith Rovers when I wanted a man with experience, a leader on the park. My first gate was 694 – so small that the tannoy announcer could just as well have read out the names of the crowd prior to the match – so we had to employ good housekeeping. Alan was not a great passer but he was a talker and a winner, a real character and a hard nut. He was also a tremendous joker in the dressing-room and the players all called him "Wingco" because he wore a leather pilot-type jacket. Actually, he reminded me of Russ Abbot.

In contrast, by 1989 we were able to make an initial six-figure down payment against the £600,000 transfer of Istvan Kozma and £200,000 on George O'Boyle, both from crack French club Bordeaux. You could not buy a player of Istvan's class for that money in this country. He is a natural athlete with phenomenal ball skills – have you ever watched him playing keepie-uppie before a game? – and can play anywhere. Sometimes the tough, physical

164

Craig Robertson scores against Dundee, March 1988

nature of Scottish football means there are games that pass him by but when he is allowed to play he shows the talent that won him all those caps for Hungary and caused our press men to write that he would have walked into our World Cup squad. Off the park Istvan is also a great prankster despite his initial difficulties in mastering the English language! Once, before a match, he left a booby-trap lighter in the dressing-room, knowing I was the only one who smoked. I, of course, picked it up and it exploded. My heart was still fluttering from that when Istvan offered me a con- ciliatory stick of chewing gum. As I reached to take it from the packet a trap sprung and trapped my finger! I think Istvan suddenly discovered a few new Lochgelly words!

George O'Boyle has quite frightening potential and is going to be a great player. His level of consistency was outstanding and, oh, the relief when he bagged that first goal at Hamilton! Sometimes fans will get on at a striker who cannot score but the supporters were aware of his unselfish play and the sheer number of goals he was creating. George did not know where Dunfermline was when

Mark Smith – faster than the speed of light

I first tried to entice him to the club. Now he knows just how big the club is.

A player doesn't have to cost a fortune to be a huge success though. Take Ross Jack, signed from Dundee for £15,000. I've probably had more rows with him than any other player. His greatest problem is that he is an awful worrier who too easily lacks confidence, but on the pitch he can be lethal. Last season's goal tally of 21 which left McCoist, Johnston, Houchen, Coyne, Djakanowski etc trailing in his wake after the previous season's astonishing 18 showed my faith in him was well placed.

Mark Smith, Graeme Robertson and Grant Tierney have all gone now but Mark could have been the greatest winger ever if he'd had the accuracy to ally to the electric pace. In Graeme we had as good an attacking full-back as you can get and he will help Partick's promotion campaign. I'll never forget his great performance in the Cup at left-back against Aberdeen. And Grant was probably the best centre-back in Division One when we signed him. He was the only part-timer in the Premier League but was magnificent in the air and a strong tackler. Only his distribution was suspect. He was a nice guy, but an excellent job with Scottish Power precluded him going full-time. He was my Man of the Match in the Skol Cup-tie with Hibs.

So many players contributed to the "Leishman era". People like Forrest, Young, Donnelly, Irvine, Hamilton, Heddle, Jenkins, Reid, Whyte, Kirkwood, T. Smith, Cowie, Ferguson, Sharp, Irons, Farningham, P. Smith, Rafferty, Nicholl, J. Donnelly, Wilson. I thank them all. We've got some great memories, lads!

Chapter 10

JIM UNLEASHED!

This is an ode to the Premier League
Jim Leishman's footballing rap
We'll talk big names and wonderful games
And some that were absolute cra..ckers

The 'Gers have Tel and Coisty and Mo
And others they're so very proud of
But are you like me, just waiting to see
What they'll nickname Comrade Kuznetsov

McNeill's in charge of things at Parkhead
The fans say that Caesar's real good
But out in Larkhall, he ain't liked at all
To King Billy, they're terribly rude

Poor Hibs got no solace from Wallace
Yet they managed to scupper his plan
When it comes to hot air, I felt I was rare
But Mercer of Hearts is your man

I hope Jim McLean will not take offence
At my efforts to do this in rhyme
I know for a fact, he puts on an act
He doesn't think laughing's a crime

Back over West, brother Tommy's in charge
Of the team in claret and amber
They once were so bold, or so I am told
To go for Gascoigne – not Paul, but Bamber

In the City of Granite, the folks it is said
Don't like to part with their cash much
Perhaps that's why, when wee Alex doth buy
The Dons always seem to go Dutch

Now the Top Ten has two sets of Saints
Who both plan to go marching in
At all-seater Perth, you're sure of a berth
Unless you're name's Gudmundur Torfasson
(OK – YOU get something to rhyme with Torfasson)

And so to East End, a place I still love
As boss there I played a star's role
Alas it's no more, I walked out the door
It's not players I sign now, just the dole

THERE are a number of topics I have touched on in my review of the Leishman era and now I would like to tie up a few loose ends. Having spent numerous matches sitting in the stand directing a game with a walkie-talkie (Gregor always used to maintain he could hear me without it anyway when I got excited!) it is surely apt to comment on referees. Like managers they are a necessity in the game and both are human. We all make mistakes. However, on a match day the fans are neither interested in the manager or the ref. The game is all about the players and a good ref won't even be noticed!

Referees can be motivated by the crowd and the atmosphere just as much as the players. Although naturally it is the most experienced refs who get the biggest matches, I am not convinced that there should be Premier, Division One and Division Two refs. Yes, it may be strange for them to go from a major Premier game with a passionate 25,000 crowd to a midweek game where there are 150 fans standing huddled in the rain but it must always be remembered that their decision will be just as vital at a Division Two or Junior game. The people organising the game at that level or involved watching or playing are every bit as passionate about their side. Neither, incidentally, am I in favour of full-time refs on high salaries.

Standards today are probably better than they have ever been and refs are very fit. The problem is that the fans find it impossible to view a referee's performance objectively. We all want to see our side do well and the ref does not have the advantage of umpteen instant replays. He has to make a decision and then stand by it. On occasion he will be wrong. All the refs I have ever spoken to have admitted crucial mistakes at one stage or another. No one is perfect. What I would like to see is the situation you have in England where linesmen have a much bigger say in a game. The ref would still have the final say but there could be more consultation. To see a player chopped down in front of a linesman and the flag staying down is remarkable but we have all seen it happen. There is only a small percentage of errors in a game but they could be further reduced.

Some managers have commented that the report system on a ref's performance is a waste of time but I feel it is important because you have an input to the game. Of course if you feel there have been 30 incidents in a game and most have gone against you, the temptation is to write the report in the heat of the moment and you would end up being destructive. It would only be seen as sour grapes in any case. However it is important to be constructive and do it a short time later. Then you tick off a number of criteria, such as co-ordination with linesmen, fitness and performance and you can write a paragraph of remarks. If you did have strong feelings you could contact the Referees' Association. However, maybe someone other than the manager ought to do the club's written report.

A referee does not tell you at half time why he has made a certain decision but some will after a game when things have calmed down and the Press and supervisors are gone! As I've said, the best refs are the ones you don't notice. Who could name me the referee at the classic Eintracht versus Real Madrid game? The fans want to see the players, the skill, the excitement, flair and imagination, not to end up bawling inanely at the man in black.

The two refs I most admire are Bob Valentine and Brian McGinlay. Bob was always very fair and once I was speaking after dinner about refs when I said, "I'm sure, lads, you'll all agree, Bob Valentine was the worst when you played in Dundee. Before the game he would shout 'Come away, United', and I just thought the bugger was short sighted!" I saw Brian McGinlay from being a youngster and he has always been extremely impressive. His standards were always of the highest and he is a great communicator. He has a great way with players and makes remarks like "On yer bike" or "You aren't doing that well either!" He appreciates the

170

Courtesy of Malky McCormick

tension and passion and is superb at taking the heat out of an incident. At the same time, he has good discipline and allows the game to flow. He is not affected by the roar of the crowd. I once wrote a few lines about him: "Right, lads, the ref today, his name is Brian. Like you boys he'll be out there trying to give the fans entertainment of the very best, to play to a high standard is all we request."

Some fans, however, do believe the refs are swayed, especially in moments of tension at Ibrox and Parkhead. It is not so true as it used to be although I concede that, as a player, the thought was often in my mind. It is only human nature and if it were a close game and a decision went against you, it was very frustrating.

Of course I am no saint in the eyes of the refs and I have experienced touchline bans. The SFA may in fact want to get rid of some of the frustration and relieve the tension. Managers, and I include myself, do over-react at times. I was bad myself on occasion and gave dog's abuse. My time in the stand gave me ample opportunity to contemplate on that and I was totally wrong! Maybe refs and managers should get together regularly, say once a month rather than once or twice a year because at present there is only time

171

to discuss negative aspects. The Managers/Coaches Association is a step in the right direction because we can work together on a code of conduct and decide that certain actions are taboo. It would also be good if refs could talk to the public about a game after a certain length of time so that the key decisions could be explained. More often than not the refs would be seen to have made the right decision.

Some managers do not like the idea of the supervisor sitting in the stand examining all the referee does, but I do. Any job has pressure and you have to be able to overcome that if you want to get to the top of the tree.

Anyway, Pars fans do know of my main misdemeanours. At Stenhousemuir early in the 1984-85 season we had gone seven games without defeat. It was a game we had to win. The match got underway and it soon became obvious that it was not going to be one of our better days. Probably as a result of this, I over-reacted to what I saw as a whole series of bad refereeing decisions by Louis Thow. Halfway through the second half I really felt that I could take no more and told the nearby linesman in no uncertain fashion just what I thought of the referee. The linesman, of course, immediately brought my remarks to the referee's attention and he summoned me to the touchline. I saw red at this point and quite simply refused to leave the dugout.

As the referee approached the dugout the crowd reacted and a barrage of coins hailed down on him like a proverbial Fife "scoor oot"! I didn't know whether to concentrate on picking up the money to help pay for what would undoubtedly be a hefty fine or to continue the argument with Louis. If I'd known then just how much I was to be fined I probably would have picked up the coins!

At the end of the game the Pars fans congregated at the Ochilview players' tunnel where Louis and the two other officials had to run the gauntlet. Some physical contact certainly took place and Louis was more than shaken by the time he reached the safety of his dressing-room. Having calmed down by that time and realising the possible repercussions of my hot temper, I approached him and apologised sincerely both for my disgraceful behaviour and for that of the Dunfermline supporters. I honestly felt that I had let both myself and the team down badly by letting my emotions run so high. Such is the passion in football, though, that it is often difficult to control yourself. Fortunately, Louis never bore a grudge and subsequently refereed well in many of our games.

In fact that particular week was a crazy one from my point of view, for a few days before, at a midweek reserve match against East Fife, I had been involved in yet another red-card incident! Dave Clarke was East Fife's manager then and still played in their second team. His tackle on Grant Jenkins was one of the worst I have ever seen and, thinking the referee was not going to take any action, possibly because Dave was manager, I completely lost the rag. A linesman became embroiled in the slagging and I was sent off. When later I read the SFA report in a much calmer mood I was ashamed of the words I had used. It struck me that the teacher who had got me my Higher Grade in English, would not have been too proud either. That's football, feelings do run high when the adrenalin starts to flow.

A number of laws are about to change and I think they are for the better. In theory the new offside law, which refs are beginning to implement, is good for the game and it will give the forward an advantage. My one concern is that teams may react by getting their defences to go deeper and that would be negative. Then there is the professional foul where a player has broken away and is almost certain to score but is pulled down. The Premier Division is all about winning, failure means you get relegated, so these things do happen. Last season in the final match Ian Westwater did the minimum required to stop John Collins of Hibs scoring and he was booked. He would now be sent off. By the same token I can think of two instances when George O'Boyle was also clean through and goalies brought him down. I do agree with the new ruling – sport is to be enjoyed and that type of foul is hindering the entertainment. The tackle from behind has also got to be stamped out because it restricts the ball player like Kozma and O'Boyle and these players must be given protection. However while we've got to get back to concentrating on the skill factor we must never lose sight of the fact that it is a man's game, a physical contact sport and we do not want to end up like a bunch of ballet dancers. The game can be both hard but fair.

I do not go along with the idea, which is very much in vogue, about players who argue resulting in the ball being moved so many yards further back for the free kick or whatever. The ref should be in control and he can book if there is dissent. Book a player often enough and that will lead to suspension and an effect on his standard of living. I have no time for gamesmanship – players wasting eight or nine minutes in a game they are winning knowing few refs play more than three or four minutes of time added on. The Cyprus verses Scotland World Cup game was a breath of fresh air in that respect and it made a distinct impact on our refs. Then there are substitutes right on the final whistle which use up a few precious seconds and the team which substitutes using the trick that the player coming off moves as far away from the dugout as he can so that the walk off uses up time. I also have no time for the player who takes a dive or feigns injury to get a fellow professional into trouble. He too has a mortgage and often a family. Any player of mine doing that would be roasted!

To some extent this gamesmanship in all its different forms stems from the pressure of the Premier Division. Jim McLean at Dundee United has never made a secret of the fact that he does not like the set up because of the cut-throat atmosphere which exists between managers, coaches and players – the people whose jobs depend on staying in that Division – with the result that we all become more defensively minded than we should be. To slip out of the League can sometimes mean a downhill descent towards obscurity.

When the Premier League began it was a necessity. There were far too many meaningless games, the Old Firm made a habit of massacring the minnows and crowds were voting with their feet. It has been a big improvement as the almost unique increases in crowds would testify. Week in week out the fans see the top clubs (albeit too often) and the top internationalists who have become household names. However I agree with Jim Farry that the time is now ripe to set up a top division of 16 teams. There is currently a whole crop of ambitious clubs out with the Premier League – Ayr, Airdrie, Kilmarnock, Falkirk, Dundee, Partick, Hamilton – who are or would go full-time and who are planning stadia which will grace the 21st century. It would reduce the number of games played at long last to 30, thereby benefiting players in European competition and those who play for Scotland, and it would allow a club like Dunfermline to consolidate. There would be much-needed scope to develop skills and nurture young talent. Last season we would have liked to have brought on our young starlets but only had the one match, the last one, where we could do that – and just look at the impact Chris Sinclair made!

Chris is the son of the sixties' star Jackie and I will always talk nostalgically of the 1960s because we just don't have the Baxters, Edwards, Johnstones or Hendersons any more. Until we get back to basics with more emphasis on skills rather than competition, young lads will never make the progress they should. It's so much nonsense when a boy of nine or ten says he is a striker or defender. Andy Roxburgh is an outstanding coach but did not have the class of players of World Cups in the past to choose from. Isn't that the fault of our Premier Division? Players on the continent have far superior ball skills.

Another change in my time at East End has been contracts. I can remember the days as a player when we all got precisely the same wage and bonus. At the end of the season we had all contributed to promotion so there was an identical cash incentive. Those days went after we got promotion to the Premier League and then began doing well in Cups. We wanted to attract a higher standard of player but these guys had a much higher basic wage and, if we were to attract them, we had to match that. Some were internationalists after all. This is how the Old Firm, Liverpool and Man United all operate. We do not compete with their wages, of course, but, like them, no two players are on identical salaries, there are the usual incentives from number of wins and playing a certain number of games. Wages at East End were always fair and the directors always consulted with me on this. It is strictly private what each player receives and this will depend on a whole variety of factors like experience, consistency and caps. There was never any disharmony over contracts even when one player would be receiving publicity during his negotiations. As we attracted a higher standard of player so there was naturally more success. The bonus for a particular result would be the same for each player and they got more for beating the likes of Dundee and St Mirren, which were so crucial, than they would for defeating the likes of the Old Firm. There was no additional money, for example, the evening we went top after the win at Fir Park. Having said that, I've never known a player yet who was discussing cash before a game. All they were bothered about was the team's performance and what they contributed. A bonus would be talked about later.

We will never be able to compete financially with the really top clubs like Rangers but we must endeavour to utilise our facilities to the maximum so we can get the most out of our resources.

Rangers have increased standards all round, improved gates, increased the glamour with their big name stars and done us all good. The coming of freedom of contract has allowed players to negotiate a new and better one once their time is up but, if they do decide to leave, their proposed new club has to deal with you. That is when the player can get his signing-on fee and improved terms. I look forward to 1992 in the sense that Dunfermline Athletic have the potential and facilities to be among the top six clubs in Scotland and therefore more quality players are going to be attracted here.

Free transfers were not normally a problem, at least not as much as I first feared. That was because often you were doing the boy a favour by letting him find his own standard and of course it made it easier for the club to progress. It was not so easy to free the sort of player whom you knew had given his all for the club or a young player who might be devastated. I never looked forward to it. When I became manager the club was still haunted by the Doug Considine affair, a player the club had signed from Aberdeen for a then colossal £43,000, only to see him drift out of the game. So from the start I had to balance the books. This got easier as time wore on because crowds got larger, more cash came in and, with the club becoming more commercially aware, the Centenary Club was funded. Sometimes my transfers just did not work, though. There was Derek O'Connor who came from Hearts. I knew he was a good pro, had high standards, would be great in the dressing-room and so on, but it just didn't work on the park. He was part of the move which brought Ian Campbell to East End Park. I thought John Donnelly would be a great success as well. He had tremendous athleticism and, if he had concentrated on football and we had pulled together, he had great potential, but it did not work that way. Willie Callaghan was given more chances than any other player, perhaps because he was the son of a famous Dunfermline player whom I had known. I admit there is a different pressure when you sign players like Willie and Chris Sinclair, Jackie's son, because with them being related to former club stars you cannot help but make comparisons. It is harder to step back and see the boy as he really is.

I've said in this book that "there is no one who managed Jim Leishman". I learned how to manage through just such trial and error as this. However I have gained experience from some other managers in one way or another. Eddie Hunter has the same passion for his club as I have for Dunfermline, and I admire enormously what he achieves at Queen's Park. Craig Brown had a considerable influence on my career when I was very much serving my apprenticeship. Alex Smith has always taken time out to guide and advise, while you must always listen to Billy McNeill, a man who learned from the master, Jock Stein. Frank Connor motivated me more than most and is determined that Raith Rovers should emulate Dunfermline. You can sit down with John Lambie to have what should be a 15-minute chat and it ends up taking 15 hours. He's a man from a similar background as mine and has been immensely successful. Graeme Souness I admire as a man who has a goal and then will do everything in his power to attain it. I might not always agree with Jim McLean's methods but there is no denying his phenomenal achievements at Dundee United and I've often said that what they have done must be the goal for the Pars. I have a lot of time for Ally McLeod, a person with a similar personality. Many have criticised him but everyone ought to have the ambition to achieve what he did and become manager of Scotland.

As we move into the 1990s one significant change is going to be in the area of stadia. There has been a lot of speculation that Dunfermline Athletic might move from East End to Pitreavie. The suggestion is that there would be a multi-million pound, purpose-built, all-seated 25,000 stadium. The money would come by selling East End, which is on a prime site in a rapidly expanding town at a time when land in that area is at a premium. The club would have a mini-Ibrox, like St Johnstone have, only larger. There would be an administration block, huge car park and an adjoining leisure complex for training facilities and a host of other sports for the local community, rather like you find on the continent. Now I am as much a fan of East End as the next man, but this is the way forward. Such a stadium would have excellent access, it would be under cover, there would be comfortable seats, modern toilets and good snacks. More families would be enticed back to the game.

The Criminal Justice Act has considerably reduced the violence and drunkenness of a decade ago and we are more safety conscious today as a result of the Popplewell Enquiry and the Taylor Report. Sometimes the Government has over-reacted to disasters yet there have also been some excellent proposals. However, a visit to a sports stadium in North America surely points the way ahead. It is ironic that Dunfermline Athletic spent £250,000 improving safety features on the terracing only to learn that, in due course, the ground must become all-seated. There will always be a place in my view for part of a ground to have terracing. A packed terracing always had a special atmosphere all of its own and why shouldn't the miner, bricklayer and joiner stand, if they wish, to shout on their favourite team?

However, the same view applies to Hampden. True, I have special memories of the place as many fans, players and managers do but Scotland needs a brand new stadium with excellent motorway access for the next century. Hampden is simply in the wrong place. Do you remember how St Johnstone fans first reacted to the news that they were to see the end of their beloved Muirton Park? Their views are now totally different – even the older ones – and the additional comforts of McDiarmid Park have seen a significant increase in gates.

Modern stadia will be part and parcel of the 1990s and so, similarly, will satellite television be. The game is becoming more commercialised now and with the high increase in wages, football clubs need all the revenue thay can get. BSB are putting a great deal of money into the Scottish game although the punters are going to find it strange initially watching a match on a Friday evening or whenever. In many ways the outcome could again emulate the experience of North America where sport has no lack of income from the media but crowds have dwindled. Who is going to go miles in driving rain to some match when they can watch their team in the comfort of their lounge? At the same time clubs in England have talked of banning away fans because they are so concerned with violence. As satellite television covers more games, "live" matches may end up only being watched by home fans. One thing is certain – nothing can ever equal the passion, excitement or all round vision which being at a game entails.

Just as when I speak to the media I do try to avoid the managerial fault of falling into the cliché trap, at the end of the day I'd like to be over the moon and not sick as a parrot – see what I mean? In saying that I am sure we are all tired of "Pars unleashed" or "Par for the course" type headlines too. One reporter said I got round it by saying 15 sentences where one word would have sufficed! I want to finish my book by talking about meeting people and in particular the fans.

I have met many people in my 22 years at East End and some would give the impression that the game is a rat race and has been poisoned. I have hardly ever experienced that. All I've met are people who believed that their particular team is best and who have supported them financially in some way. There is only a small minority of rats. The fans and the players are the people who really count and that is why, like many others, I was so concerned about the proposed take-over of Hibs. Scotland could not afford to lose such a big club while the Capital is well able to support two big teams. The reality is that most Hibs fans and indeed many Hearts fans would not have supported the new merged club. What was needed was a superstadium where the two clubs could have played alternatively, Milan-style, and retained their identities. The fans were the last people to be considered.

At Dunfermline during my managerial reign that was never the case. Dunfermline was their club, not mine or that of the directors, but theirs. Until July 1990 I never dreamed that I could have more feelings for them than I already had but the letters, telphone calls and demonstrations just overwhelmed me. There are three particular fond memories I have of them. First, that gala day when we drew 3-3 in a magnificent opening Premier League game with Hibernian. As the team ran down the steps the ovation was thunderous and when the players ran to the centre of the field to applaud the fans, it was a mutual recognition of all the hard work that had been put in for so long to get us back at the top. We were actually playing in the Premier League at last.

Then there was the last match of that season when we lost 1-0 at Celtic as they were celebrating their centenary. A large banner stated "Happy birthday Celtic and we'll be back!" I had warned my team beforehand to be professional, play to their own high standards and try to spoil the party. They were to try to avoid getting caught up in the emotion of it all. In the event it was me who did, especially when the legions of wonderful Celtic fans chanted my name. I had learned another managerial lesson.

Finally, there was that day in May 1989 when we secured the First Division Championship. Running round the track in celebration, I had never felt closer to the fans. We had shared something together, something that we had never achieved before. Again, it wasn't my team or the directors' team, it was our team. Perhaps that is the whole point of this book. It is very rewarding when people have called me Mr Dunfermline but no one person is bigger than the club. Only the fans are!

The JIM LEISHMAN Record
1983-1990
Compiled by Duncan Simpson

PLAYING CAREER

Jim Leishman was snapped up by Andy Young while playing for Townhill Boys Club in 1968. He went on to win Scottish Schoolboy caps and was called up as a player on 3 June 1971.

Jim made his first team debut on 18 September 1971, still only aged 17. Confronted with injuries to George O'Neill, Jim Brown and Pat Gardner, manager Alex Wright decided to gamble on playing his young defender in midfield for a potentially difficult game against Ayr United at Somerset Park. It worked because Dunfermline secured an important 1-1 draw and Jim's performance was praised by both his manager and by captain John Cushley.

Although Jim's appearances were limited in his first season, he did manage to score two goals. His first came on Saturday, 22 April 1972 in a League match against Clyde at East End Park. Wearing the number six shirt, Jim went up for a corner and headed Dunfermline's second goal into the net in 62 minutes. Five days later, on Thursday, 27 April 1972, Jim scored what could well be the finest ever goal by a Dunfermline player at Ibrox. With the score at 3-3, Jim took the ball in the inside-right position, then beat two defenders before crashing a left-foot shot off the inside of the post past goalkeeper Peter McCloy to give Dunfermline a rare win against Rangers in Glasgow.

Dunfermline's long-serving full-back Willie Callaghan was released in September 1972, thus paving the way for Jim Leishman to win a regular first team place. He was a member of the Pars promotion-winning side of 1972-73, and retained his place the following season as Dunfermline consolidated their place back in the top League.

On 21 August 1974, Dunfermline played Hearts in a League Cup tie at Tynecastle. At approximately 7.50 p.m., Jim and Hearts player Jim Jeffries had a terrible collision. Jim's leg was broken in three places and from that moment his career was virtually ended. Jim was only 20 at the time and it is strange to think that he might still have been playing football today had it not happened.

Jim's recovery was slow but he was eventually given another last chance to play for Dunfermline. On 18 February 1976, the then manager Harry Melrose brought Jim on as a substitute for the last 15 minutes of a League match against Clyde. Even then Jim's appearance was greeted with great applause by the fans, but Jim and everyone else knew that his playing days were over.

In 1976 he went to Cowdenbeath in a player-swop with Bobby Morrison, but after one season and only 11 first-team appearances Jim had left to play junior football with Glenrothes. After six months, Jim gave up playing altogether.

Jim returned to playing in 1978, but this time with additional responsibilities. As player/coach with Oakley, it was to be an introduction to the side of the game which he was to prove very adept at.

EARLY DAYS IN MANAGEMENT

In 1980, Jim became manager of Kelty Hearts, then later that year Andy Rolland took him back to Central Park as a coach. His services were dispensed with when Rolland resigned and Hugh Wilson took over.

On 23 July 1982, Pat Stanton brought Jim back to East End Park to take charge of the youth team. Under Tom Forsyth, he was promoted to Reserve Team Coach.

On Monday, 17 October 1983, Tom Forsyth resigned as manager after a 1-0 home defeat by Arbroath. Control was handed over to Jim on a caretaker basis, and within 24 hours of taking charge the Reserves defeated Queen's Park Reserves 3-0.

Jim's first statement as manager was: "I see it as my job for the moment to getting the players going again and getting the team back in the running in time for a new manager taking over. I've decided I'm going to enjoy myself and take it from there. I hope I can get some of my enthusiasm for this club over to the players."

Still as caretaker manager, Jim made his first signings. On 25 October 1983 he signed Ian Heddle from Dunfermline Railway Club, and the following day he signed Allan Forsyth from Raith Rovers.

Jim's first team selection as manager was for the game against Queen's Park on 22 October 1983. The team was: Whyte, Crawford, Lapsley, Wilcox, Dall, Donnelly, Simpson, McCathie, Morrison, Perry, Jenkins; subs: Forrest and Black. Dunfermline lost 3-1, with Grant Jenkins scoring the first goal with Leishman as manager.

After considering 40 applications, the Board decided to offer the manager's post to Jim Leishman on 31 October 1983. He was the first part-time manager since the war.

184

HOUSE OF DISTINCTION
AND QUALITY
BUILDING CONTRACTORS

Wm. RENNIE

& CO. LTD.
GOWKHALL JOINERY
WORKS
Carnock Road
Dunfermline
Tel. — New Oakley 402

Sponsors of Dunfermline Athletic

Jim's first win as manager came on 5 November 1983 when a Steve Morrison goal was enough to earn both points at Montrose.

The first players to leave East End Park after Jim took over were Derek Rodier who was transferred to Berwick, and Jim Moffat who went to Forfar. In the meantime, one of Leishman's earliest signings, John Watson, was making a name for himself scoring five goals in four reserve outings.

MANAGERS

The record of Jim Leishman can be compared to Dunfermline's other managers as follows:

Manager	Tenure	P	W	D	L	F	A	Success
William Knight (1st spell) (3 years 79 days)	13.03.22 – 31.05.25	128	44	33	51	175	160	47.3%
Sandy Paterson (5 years)	31.05.25 – 31.05.30	199	4	33	92	387	433	45.5%
William Knight (2nd spell) (5 years 363 days)	31.05.30 – 28.05.36	231	107	38	86	489	440	54.5%
David Taylor (1 year 309 days)	05.06.36 – 10.04.38	75	22	17	36	147	176	40.7%
Peter Wilson (1 year 27 days)	04.05.38 – 31.05.39	38	20	6	12	109	84	60.5%
Sandy Archibald (7 years 38 days)	12.10.39 – 19.11.46	192	91	25	76	443	410	53.9%
Wm McAndrew (199 days)	13.02.47 – 31.08.47	12	5	0	7	23	39	41.7%
Bobby Calder (162 days)	01.09.47 – 9. 2.48	23	5	4	14	46	59	30.4%
Webber Lees (2 years)	31.07.49 – 01.08.51	90	39	10	31	173	170	48.9%
Bobby Ancell (3 years)	01.08.52 – 31.07.55	115	51	24	40	233	210	54.8%

Manager	Tenure	P	W	D	L	F	A	Success
Andy Dickson (4 years 206 days)	01.08.55 – 22.02.60	210	80	40	90	437	436	47.6%
Jock Stein (4 years 16 days)	14.03.60 – 30.03.64	192	93	37	62	397	280	58.1%
Wm Cunningham (3 years 83 days)	30.03.64 – 22.06.67	162	89	34	39	368	216	65.4%
George Farm (3 years 75 days)	17.07.67 – 01.10.70	157	70	28	59	248	222	53.5%
Alex Wright (1 year 122 days)	22.10.70 – 21.02.72	63	12	19	32	66	94	34.1%
George Miller (3 years 191 days)	22.02.72 – 31.08.75	146	50	36	60	236	235	46.6%
Harry Melrose (5 years 80 days)	20.09.75 – 09.12.80	232	86	72	74	300	291	52.6%
Pat Stanton (1 year 267 days)	16.12.80 – 02.09.82	72	19	19	34	74	115	39.6%
Tom Forsyth (1 year 45 days)	20.09.82 – 17.10.83	49	11	18	20	51	82	40.8%
Jim Leishman (6 years 256 days)	17.10.83 – Present	302	128	77	97	431	373	55.1%

Correct at 30.06.90

MANAGERIAL SUCCESS

It is extremely difficult to gauge managerial success since each manager is confronted with different conditions and opportunities. Having said that, there can be no doubt that Jim is among the most successful of all Dunfermline's managers. In strict percentage terms, Jim comes fourth on the list behind Willie Cunningham (65.4%), Peter Wilson (60.5%), and Jock Stein (58.1%). Wilson can be discounted since his managerial term was only one season – not really long enough for a fair assessment. Willie Cunningham's three-year term was highly successful, but despite coming within a whisker of completing a League and Cup double in 1965, he

187

finished without ever having won a trophy. It was also said – probably unkindly – that Cunningham's success was mainly due to the good side which he had inherited from Jock Stein. The same could certainly not be said about Stein himself who took over a team which was hurtling towards the Second Division. Just over one year later his team had won the Scottish Cup. It is for this reason that Stein is generally considered to be Dunfermline's best manager.

There are, strangely enough, quite a few parallels between Stein and Leishman. Jim also inherited a poor side – possibly the worst in terms of playing ability that the club has ever had – but he too was able to wave a magic wand and within a very short space of time had a team competing in the top ten. What is more, Jim did win things – two League Championships for a start. There is no doubt that the fans see Jim as up there running neck and neck with Stein for the accolade of Dunfermline's best.

TENURE

At 30 June 1990, Jim Leishman had already passed a number of records. As manager for six years and 256 days he had already long passed the previous post-war record of Harry Melrose. He is only a short few months away from the all-time record for a single spell which is held by Sandy Archibald. His term of seven years and 38 days occurred during the war period and is therefore of less significance. Dunfermline's longest serving manager was William Knight who held the hot seat for a total of nine years and 77 days in two spells from 1922-1925 and 1930-1936.

Jim's 302 games in charge is the greatest number by any manager except Knight who took charge of 359 games. Similarly, Jim's 128 wins was only surpassed by Knight. Jim has one record all to himself – his teams have drawn 77 games!

ATTENDANCES

Jim Leishman will be known as the manager who brought the crowds flocking back to East End Park. There may have been a slight general upturn in attendances in Scotland, but this cannot disguise the incredible increases seen at Dunfermline. At the end of the season in which Jim first took over, a *total* of 20,706 spectators

188

watched Dunfermline's home League matches for an average of 1,090 per game. In season 1989-90, Dunfermline's home League games had been watched by no fewer than 197,804 – an average of 10,989 per game. This represents an increase of over 1,000% in seven seasons!

For those who consider that these figures are only due to having 'Old Firm' fans around to boost the numbers, then here are a few more figures to ponder:

★ Dunfermline's attendances in 1989-90 were the *fifth* highest in Scotland, with only Rangers, Celtic, Hearts and Aberdeen attracting more. It is the first time in history that Dunfermline have attracted more spectators over a season that Hibernian.

★ On 7 April 1984, Dunfermline's home League match against Arbroath attracted a total of 358 spectators – East End Park's lowest-known crowd for a League match. On 13 May 1989, Dunfermline's League match against Meadowbank – a team of roughly the same drawing power as Arbroath – was watched by 12,976 spectators.

★ Since Jim Leishman became manager, Dunfermline's crowds have been consistently higher than both teams which are higher placed and teams from bigger centres of population.

Dunfermline's home League attendances for the period 1983 to 1990 were as follows on page 190.

PLAYERS

During his seven years in charge Jim has used a total of 90 players in official matches. Dunfermline's longest serving player Norrie McCathie has been involved in 268 of the 300 games which Jim Leishman has taken charge of, while John Watson and Ian Westwater have also played in more than 200.

Jim's most used substitute has been Trevor Smith, although Stevie Morrison and Grant Jenkins also spent a fair amount of time on the sub's bench.

GOALSCORERS

Jim has managed to unearth some exciting goalscorers in his time, and most of them have come for the equivalent, in footballing terms, of "peanuts".

THE JIM LEISHMAN RECORD ATTENDANCES

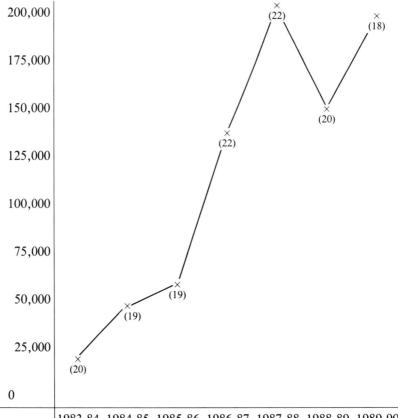

1983-84 1984-85 1985-86 1986-87 1987-88 1988-89 1989-90
Number of home games in brackets

Three men in particular stand out:

★ John Watson, probably Jim's most famous signing, was bought from Hong Kong Rangers for £300. He went on to score 85 goals with Dunfermline to become one of the club's all-time top goalscorers. In 1985-86 he was top goalscorer in Scotland with 31 goals, winning the *Daily Record* Golden Shot Award.

★ Ross Jack, signed from Dundee for £15,000 in 1987, has scored 45 goals up to the start of the 1990-91 season. At a rate of one goal for every 2.51 games, he has a slightly higher strike rate than Watson and considering that his opposition has generally been of a higher standard, his is a considerable achievement. In 1988-89 he was sixth highest goalscorer in Scotland and won the SPFA First Division Player of the Year Award, while in 1989-90 he was the second highest goalscorer in the Premier League.

★ Craig Robertson, signed from Raith Rovers for £25,000, had a tremendous strike rate (3.32), despite being a midfielder. In 1987-88 he was Dunfermline's top goalscorer and that season, despite Dunfermline's relegation, finished as the top goalscoring midfielder in the Premier League.

Of the 82 outfield players employed by Jim, 37 did not manage to score for Dunfermline. Among the most notable among them are the late Gary Riddell, and current players Ray Farningham and Raymond Sharp.

Player	Goals Scored	Player	Scored
Watson, John	85	Callaghan, Willie	2
Jack, Ross	45	Gallacher, Eddie	2
Jenkins, Grant	37	Holt, John	2
McCathie, Norrie	29	Irvine, Willie	2
Morrison, Stephen	28	Moyes, David	2
Campbell, Ian	19	Rougvie, Doug	2
Robertson, Craig	19	Tait, Gavin	2
Smith, Trevor	18	Thompson, Gary	2
Ferguson, Eric	10	Abercromby, Billy	1
McCall, Ian	10	Cowie, George	1
Heddle, Ian	8	Dall, Robert	1
Smith, Paul	8	Forsyth, Alan	1
Young, David	8	Lapsley, John	1
Donnelly, John	7	Liddell, Frank	1
Hamilton, Rowan	7	McGlashan, Colin	1
Perry, John	7	O'Connor, Derek	1
Smith, Mark	7	Rafferty, Stuart	1
Irons, David	6	Robertson, Bobby	1
Kozma, Istvan	6	Smith, Bobby	1
Forrest, Bobby	5	Andersen, Vetle	0
Stewart, Rab	5	Black, Graeme	0
Beedie, Stuart	4	Bonnyman, Phil	0
Bowie, James	4	Burns, Hugh	0
O'Boyle, George	4	Carson, Tom	0
Robertson, Graeme	4	Clark, Sandy	0
Tierney, Grant	3	Connolly, Gordon	0

Player	Goals Scored	Player	Goals Scored
Crawford, Paul	0	Riddell, Gary	0
Davidson, Graeme	0	Rodger, Paul	0
Docherty, Jim	0	Rodier, Derek	0
Donnelly, Paul	0	Segers, Hans	0
Dunlop, J	0	Sharp, Raymond	0
Farningham, Ray	0	Simpson, Stephen	0
Feenie, Martin	0	Sinclair, Chris	0
Gordon, Ian	0	Speirs, Gardner	0
Hepburn, Kevin	0	Strang, Shaun	0
Houston, David	0	Waddell, John	0
Irvine, Andy	0	Walker, Nicky	0
Kirkwood, Billy	0	Wardell, Stuart	0
Mackay, Billy	0	Westwater, Ian	0
McAlpine, Hamish	0	Westwood, David	0
McKellar, David	0	Whyte, Hugh	0
Nicholl, Jimmy	0	Wilcox, David	0
O'Hara, Anthony	0	Williamson, Andy	0
Pryde, Ian	0	Wilson, Gordon	0
Reid, Grant	0	Wilson, Tommy	0

Player	Scoring Rate (Games per Goal)	Player	Scoring Rate (Games per Goal)
Jack, Ross	2.51	Callaghan, Willie	8.00
Watson, John	2.52	O'Boyle, George	8.75
Campbell, Ian	2.89	O'Connor, Derek	9.00
Liddell, Frank	3.00	Smith, Mark	9.00
Robertson, Craig	3.32	McCathie, Norrie	9.24
Jenkins, Grant	4.24	Tait, Gavin	9.50
Stewart, Rab	4.80	Smith, Paul	9.87
Ferguson, Eric	5.10	Dall, Robert	11.00
McCall, Ian	5.10	Gallacher, Eddie	12.00
Donnelly, John	5.14	Hamilton, Rowan	12.00
Heddle, Ian	5.87	Lapsley, John	12.00
Kozma, Istvan	6.33	Irons, David	13.83
Perry, John	6.71	Abercromby, Billy	14.00
Smith, Trevor	6.72	Young, David	15.75
Morrison, Stephen	6.89	Cowie, George	16.00
Irvine, Willie	7.00	McGlashan, Colin	16.00

Player	Scoring Rate (Games per Goal)	Player	Scoring Rate (Games per Goal)
Rougvie, Doug	18.00	Thompson, Gary	27.50
Beedie, Stuart	18.75	Forrest, Bobby	31.00
Bowie, James	20.00	Rafferty, Stuart	40.00
Tierney, Grant	20.33	Forsyth, Alan	41.00
Moyes, David	21.50	Smith, Bobby	77.00
Robertson, Graeme	26.00	Robertson, Bobby	146.00
Holt, John	26.50		

GOALS

The folks at Starks Park won't be too happy, but Jim Leishman's teams have scored more goals against Raith Rovers than any other team, while George O'Boyle's solitary strike against Hamilton in the Scottish Cup is the only goal he has to show against Hamilton. Rangers top the goals against column, but the first team outwith the Premier League to score a lot of goals against Jim's teams is Raith Rovers, thus showing just how good value for money these local derbies have been.

In total in League, Skol and Scottish Cup matches, Jim's Pars have scored 432 goals while conceding 374.

Opposition	Goals by Dunfermline	Opposition	Goals by Dunfermline
RAITH ROVERS	24	AYR UNITED	12
ALBION ROVERS	23	DUNDEE	12
QUEEN OF THE SOUTH	21	MONTROSE	12
EAST STIRLINGSHIRE	20	MOTHERWELL	12
MORTON	20	PARTICK THISTLE	12
STRANRAER	18	HIBERNIAN	11
ARBROATH	17	STENHOUSEMUIR	11
BERWICK RANGERS	17	BRECHIN CITY	10
FORFAR ATHLETIC	15	CLYDE	10
QUEENS PARK	15	KILMARNOCK	10
COWDENBEATH	14	CELTIC	8
ST MIRREN	14	HEART OF MIDLOTHIAN	8
ST JOHNSTONE	13	RANGERS	8
STIRLING ALBION	13	EAST FIFE	7

Opposition	Goals by Dunfermline	Opposition	Goals by Dunfermline
ABERDEEN	6	CLYDEBANK	4
AIRDRIEONIANS	6	DUMBARTON	4
MEADOWBANK THISTLE	6	DUNDEE UNITED	4
ALLOA ATHLETIC	5	FALKIRK	4
THREAVE ROVERS	5	HAMILTON ACADEMICAL	1

Opposition	Goals Against Dunfermline	Opposition	Goals Against Dunfermline
RANGERS	31	ARBROATH	9
ABERDEEN	24	STENHOUSEMUIR	9
HEART OF MIDLOTHIAN	21	FALKIRK	8
HIBERNIAN	19	AIRDRIEONIANS	7
CELTIC	17	COWDENBEATH	7
MOTHERWELL	17	MONTROSE	7
QUEENS PARK	16	KILMARNOCK	6
RAITH ROVERS	16	AYR UNITED	5
EAST FIFE	13	PARTICK THISTLE	5
DUNDEE	12	ALBION ROVERS	4
MORTON	12	CLYDEBANK	4
QUEEN OF THE SOUTH	12	ALLOA ATHLETIC	3
ST MIRREN	12	BRECHIN CITY	3
STIRLING ALBION	12	CLYDE	3
BERWICK RANGERS	11	STRANRAER	3
DUNDEE UNITED	11	DUMBARTON	2
FORFAR ATHLETIC	11	ST JOHNSTON	1
MEADOWBANK THISTLE	11	HAMILTON ACADEMICAL	0
EAST STIRLINGSHIRE	10	THREAVE ROVERS	0

OPPOSITION

In his time as manager, Jim has played against every League team although he has yet to face Hamilton in a League match despite playing two full seasons in each of the three Divisions. He has also had one encounter with non-League opposition – against Threave Rovers in the Scottish Cup.

Queen of the South have provided the opposition on most occasions, with Rangers and Morton following closely after that. Most wins have come against Queen of the South and Cowdenbeath (7), most losses against Rangers (9), while after the six draws against Queen of the South, most draws have been recorded against Hibernian and Stenhousemuir (4).

Complete Record

Opposition	P	W	L	D
ABERDEEN	10	0	8	2
AIRDRIEONIANS	7	2	2	3
ALBION ROVERS	8	5	1	2
ALLOA ATHLETIC	3	1	0	2
ARBROATH	9	5	2	2
AYR UNITED	5	3	0	2
BERWICK RANGERS	8	4	1	3
BRECHIN CITY	4	3	1	0
CELTIC	11	3	6	2
CLYDE	7	4	1	2
CLYDEBANK	3	1	1	1
COWDENBEATH	9	7	1	1
DUMBARTON	4	3	1	0
DUNDEE	9	5	4	0
DUNDEE UNITED	8	0	5	3
EAST FIFE	7	1	4	2
EAST STIRLINGSHIRE	11	6	3	2
FALKIRK	7	1	4	2
FORFAR ATHLETIC	10	6	3	1
HAMILTON ACADEMICAL	2	1	0	1
HEART OF MIDLOTHIAN	10	2	8	0
HIBERNIAN	11	2	5	4
KILMARNOCK	7	3	1	3
MEADOWBANK THISTLE	6	1	2	3
MONTROSE	10	5	2	3
MORTON	12	6	3	3
MOTHERWELL	9	2	4	3
PARTICK THISTLE	7	6	0	1
QUEEN OF THE SOUTH	15	7	2	6
QUEENS PARK	9	3	3	3
RAITH ROVERS	11	6	3	2
RANGERS	12	1	9	2
ST JOHNSTONE	6	6	0	0
ST MIRREN	9	5	3	1

We've been in
football as long as
their sleeves!

umbro

Opposition	P	W	L	D
STENHOUSEMUIR	9	2	3	4
STIRLING ALBION	8	3	2	3
STRANRAER	8	7	0	1
THREAVE ROVERS	1	1	0	0

League Record

Opposition	Games	Pts	Opposition	Games	Pts
ABERDEEN	8	1	HAMILTON ACADEMICAL	0	0
AIRDRIEONIANS	7	7	HEART OF MIDLOTHIAN	8	4
ALBION ROVERS	8	12	HIBERNIAN	8	6
ALLOA ATHLETIC	3	4	KILMARNOCK	7	9
ARBROATH	8	10	MEADOWBANK THISTLE	6	5
AYR UNITED	3	5	MONTROSE	10	13
BERWICK RANGERS	8	11	MORTON	11	15
BRECHIN CITY	4	6	MOTHERWELL	8	5
CELTIC	8	7	PARTICK THISTLE	7	13
CLYDE	7	10	QUEEN OF THE SOUTH	15	20
CLYDEBANK	3	3	QUEEN'S PARK	9	9
COWDENBEATH	8	13	RAITH ROVERS	9	10
DUMBARTON	4	6	RANGERS	8	2
DUNDEE	8	8	ST JOHNSTONE	6	12
DUNDEE UNITED	8	3	ST MIRREN	8	11
EAST FIFE	6	2	STENHOUSEMYIR	8	6
EAST STIRLINGSHIRE	9	12	STIRLING ALBION	8	9
FALKIRK	7	4	STRANRAER	8	15
FORFAR ATHLETIC	9	11	THREAVE ROVERS	0	0

SUCCESS RATE

Surprisingly, the team which Jim apparently cannot fail against is a club currently in the Premier League! St Johnstone have failed to take even a point against Dunfermline while Jim has been in charge at East End Park. Jim also has a good record against some so-called "bogie" teams of the past like Ayr United and local rivals Cowdenbeath.

Although Jim did have the satisfaction of leading Dunfermline into a Centenary Match win over Aberdeen, in ten League and Cup outings against the Dons his teams have failed to record a single win. His record against three of Scotland's other top clubs is not great either, but surely Jim's most dreaded opponents are East Fife and Falkirk. Both have given him much more bother than many of the Premier League teams.

Success

Opposition	Percentage Success	Opposition	Percentage Success
ST JOHNSTONE	100.00	RAITH ROVERS	63.64
THREAVE ROVERS	100.00	MORTON	62.50
STRANRAER	93.75	ST MIRREN	61.11
PARTICK THISTLE	92.86	STIRLING ALBION	56.25
COWDENBEATH	83.33	DUNDEE	55.56
AYR UNITED	80.00	AIRDRIEONIANS	50.00
ALBION ROVERS	75.00	CLYDEBANK	50.00
BRECHIN CITY	75.00	QUEENS PARK	50.00
DUMBARTON	75.00	STENHOUSEMUIR	44.44
HAMILTON ACADEMICAL	75.00	MEADOWBANK THISTLE	41.67
CLYDE	71.43	MOTHERWELL	38.89
BERWICK RANGERS	68.75	CELTIC	36.36
ALLOA ATHLETIC	66.67	HIBERNIAN	36.36
ARBROATH	66.67	EAST FIFE	28.57
QUEEN OF THE SOUTH	66.67	FALKIRK	28.57
FORFAR ATHLETIC	65.00	HEART OF MIDLOTHIAN	20.00
MONTROSE	65.00	DUNDEE UNITED	18.75
KILMARNOCK	64.29	RANGERS	16.67
EAST STIRLINGSHIRE	63.64	ABERDEEN	10.00

LEAGUE PROGRESS

Dunfermline's League record for the period 1983 to 1990 is as follows on page 199.

ACHIEVEMENTS

★ Longest undefeated run in the history of the club. Between 24 August 1985 and 26 January 1986 Dunfermline went 19 games without defeat. That run also included 17 consecutive League games without defeat – also a club record.

THE JIM LEISHMAN RECORD 1983-1990

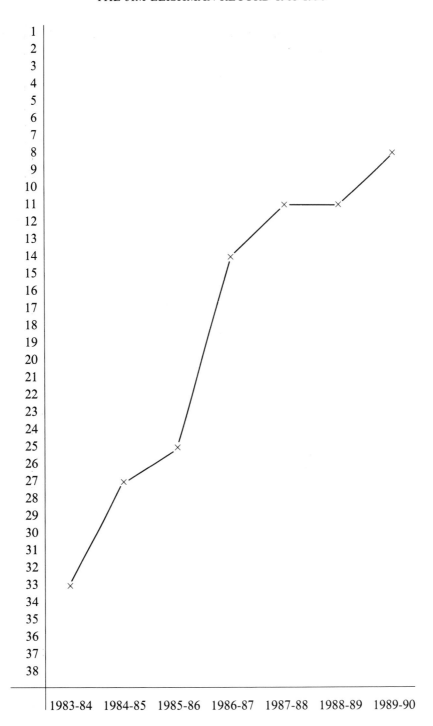

★ Longest undefeated run in the new First Division. Between 22 November 1986 and 28 February 1987 Dunfermline went 11 League games without defeat.

★ Longest undefeated run in the Premier Division. Between 23 September 1989 and 18 November 1989, Dunfermline went eight League games without defeat. During this spell, Dunfermline also went to the top of the Scottish League for the first time in the club's history.

★ Scottish Second Division Champions in 1985-86 with the highest number of League goals by any team in Britain.

★ Promoted to the Premier Division for the first time in the club's history in 1986-87. In doing so, Dunfermline became only the second club in history to go from the Second Division to the Premier in two seasons.

★ Scottish First Division Champions in 1988-89.

★ Scottish BP Youth Cup Champions in 1987-88, and Scottish Reserve League East Champions in 1986-87.

★ The first ever Dunfermline player to be capped by Scotland at under-21 level – Raymond Sharp against Norway in November 1989. Also the first young Dunfermline player to be capped by Scotland at under-age level for several years.

★ Istvan Kozma became the first Dunfermline player to win a full international cap since Geir Karlsen in 1974.

★ A new club transfer fee received – £200,000 for Ian McCall from Rangers in September 1988.

★ A new club transfer fee paid out – £540,000 for Istvan Kozma from Bordeaux in September 1989.

★ In 1987, a return to full-time football for the first time since 1976.

★ Reached the semi-final of a major competition for the first time since 1969. Also reached two other quarter-finals.

★ Defeated Celtic at Parkhead in a League game for only the second time in the club's history. Also defeated Hearts twice at Tynecastle, having only ever won there three times before.

★ The greatest ever number of Dunfermline supporters clubs established. During season 1989-90 there were 24 different supporters' clubs from all over Fife, Lothian, Central Region and Glasgow.

JIM SIGNS FULL-TIME CONTRACT

Dunfermline boss Jim Leishman yesterday put pen to paper on a two-year contract which will make him the club's first full-time manager since Harry Melrose in the mid 1970s.

Leishman, who has until now been dividing his time between both the commercial and on-field aspects of the club, committed himself to two years on a full-time basis.

"I want to become the club's longest-serving manager and hopefully this new contract will help me achieve that," said Jim.

"The contract had really nothing to do with money, that's been agreed for a long time, but I've got security as well now," he added.

Club chairman Mel Rennie explained that Jim's signing was part of the recently-announced decision to form a nucleus of full-time players at East End Park in their bid to reach the Premier League.

He said that this weekend the club, who are currently joint top of the First Division, would be advertising the post of commercial manager.

"Jim had the weekend to think things over and everybody is delighted he's staying with us because he has such a great enthusiasm," said Mr Rennie.

Leishman says he feels that with the kind of enthusiasm that exists at East End Park, the potential for achieving success is very real indeed.

"If I didn't think we could go further I wouldn't be here, but I still get a great feeling of pride being involved with Dunfermline," he said.

Courier *16.10.86*

PARS IN PERSON – JIM LEISHMAN

How could we conclude such a memorable season without having our final interview with the man with the biggest job of all? Well we almost didn't because trying to sit Jim Leishman down to talk quietly for five or ten minutes is nearly asking the impossible!

Watching him in action, you can't help but admire his style. He's happy to greet anybody no matter who they are or how insignificant they may be. He rarely gets through a conversation without telling a story or cracking a joke, yet he is serious and thoughtful when he needs to be.

After his playing career was prematurely ended it looked as if Leishman was finished with football. Slowly, but surely, he worked his way back through the ranks. His appointment as Dunfermline manager raised a few eyebrows in October 1983, but he has answered his critics by giving Dunfermline continuing success.

Players have commented on just how good a motivator he is, so is this the secret of his success or is there more? We finally got a chance to ask him . . .

Remind us of the background to your career?
I was signed as a youngster by Andy Young when George Farm was Dunfermline's manager. I played for Scottish Schoolboys, then played my first team game when Alex Wright was manager. I was a regular for the next couple of seasons until I got my leg broken in a tackle with Jim Jeffries in a League Cup match against Hearts in 1974. After I came back I couldn't get a regular place – I knew I wouldn't be the same player again. Out of frustration I went in a player swop with Bobby Morrison to Cowdenbeath – I wanted a first-team game. After a while there I went to Glenrothes for six months but then just gave up football completely for two years. I was the youngest "old crock" in the game! To be honest even winning the League Championship wouldn't completely make up for the playing career I've missed.

How did you come back into the game?
I went back to play with Oakley Juniors then managed Kelty Hearts. Andy Rolland asked me to become his assistant at Cowdenbeath, but when he resigned that was the end of that. Pat Stanton asked me to become Youth Team Coach at East End – I'll always be thankful to him for the chance he gave me. When Tom Forsyth took over I became Reserve Team Coach.

It surprised a lot of people when you got the manager's job – were you surprised to get it?
I suppose I was. When I was caretaker manager I was told just to get on with it as best I could. I worked solidly for 28 days, and although our results weren't great they must have decided to give me a try. I was just looking to hold on to my Reserve Team job.

How did you decide to operate in those early days?

I was only 29 at the time and it was difficult to make the transition to manager. I'm learning all the time and am finding it easier to make the harder decisions. At the end of the first season I freed quite a few players to make room for new signings. I also moved Bobby Forrest to full-back and Norrie McCathie to defence.

Basically I am a player's manager – I want them to be happy and would do anything in my power to keep them that way.

How do you think the season has gone?

Better than we could have imagined and nobody should take away from what has been done. At the beginning of the season the lads played with grit and determination and that got us through the first matches. In the middle we played some really good football. Lately the pressure has been getting to us but we're hanging in there.

Assuming we do enough to win that Premier League place, how do you think the team will do?

You can't assume anything – we've still got a job to do to get to the Premier League. The season is 44 games long.

If I'm pushed I would say that the Premier League is really two leagues. We would do well to finish in a good position in the lower league and keep away from relegation.

Your name has been associated with other jobs – would you move from Dunfermline?

I could have moved twice this season but turned down the chance. You can never say what circumstances will decide but I would like to stay with Dunfermline for a long time, especially as long as the players want me here.

The crowd have been giving the team a bit of stick lately. What do you think of their behaviour?

I'm very disappointed. The boys need all the support they can get right now.

For every bad supporter there are ten good ones. We're doing this for all the real supporters. I'd like to see them rallying round for the final games.

CAREER PROFILE – JIM LEISHMAN

Born: Lochgelly
Date of Birth: 15 November 1953
Height: 5ft 11½ins
Weight: Not admitted
Previous Club: Dunfermline United
First Game for Dunfermline: v. Ayr United (League) on 18.09.71
Last Game for Dunfermline: v. Clyde (as sub) on 18.02.76
Date Signed as Player: 3 June 1971
Date Became Manager: 31 October 1983

Career Record (A = Appearances; G = Goals)

	League		Lge Cup		Scot Cup		Total	
	A	G	A	G	A	G	A	G
For Dunfermline								
1971-72	6(1)	2	–	–	–	–	6(1)	2
1972-73	29(1)	1	2(1)	1	1	–	32(2)	2
1973-74	28(1)	1	8	1	4(1)	–	40(2)	2
1974-75	–	–	3	–	–	–	3	–
1975-76	0(1)	–	–	–	–	–	0(1)	–
For Cowdenbeath								
1976-77	11	–	–	–	–	–	11	–
	74(4)	4	13(1)	2	5(1)	–	92(6)	6

Appearances as substitute in brackets